Elegance in Motion

A Parkinson's Diva Journey of
Faith and Perseverance

Maria De León, MD

Published in Canton, Georgia, USA by *thewordverve LLC*
(www.thewordverve.com)

First edition 2025
Published in Canton, GA, USA, by *thewordverve* (**www.thewordverve.com**)
eBook: 978-1-956856-53-8
Paperback: 978-1-956856-55-2
Hardback: 978-1-956856-54-5
Library of Congress Control Number: 2025905709

Cover artwork by Ros Webb www.roswebbart.com
Cover and interior design by Robin Krauss www.bookformatters.com
eBook formatting by *thewordverve*

Dr. De León does it again, proving why she is the Parkinson's Diva extraordinaire. Written in her trademark flair, this book is packed with practicality and important information—and her delightful sense of humor is the cherry on top!

— *Wilma Cordova, MSW Director and professor of school social work at SFA University*

A Parkinson's diagnosis can feel like one's life has been brought to a screeching halt. De León's *Elegance in Motion* provides solace and comfort in light of these challenges. She vulnerably shares the story of her diagnosis interwoven loving and sometimes humorous portrayals of her life journey, offering context to the experience of Parkinson's disease.

— *Vanessa Reiser, filmmaker*

Reading *Elegance in Motion* connected me with my essence, my roots—who I am—as it represents all Latin women and how the love of family influences us throughout life. My parents have Parkinson's, and the process of receiving a diagnosis, accepting it, and moving forward can be quite a challenge. There are angels who are here to help us, to reaffirm our faith, and Maria De León is one of them.

— *Adriana Jiminez, director of Give For a Smile (GFAS)*

Parkinson's Diva

DEDICATION

To My God first and foremost all the glory, my love, and gratitude for
showing me mercy, grace, and forgiveness despite my
many shortcomings and unworthiness.

My devotion and affection to my wonderful daughter Victoria
and loving husband Allen, whose unconditional love
and support are the air beneath my wings.

To my mother, her constant prayers have helped me to persevere.

To my mentor, friend, and colleague, Dr. Mya Schiess

To all my wonderful friends, old and new, including my editor.

"The pearl is queen of gems and gem of queens."

— Anonymous

Diva

Di va. / ˈdi və, -va / noun.

A well-rounded female who boldly displays the five virtues: dignity, inspiration, vision, achievement, and sisterhood.

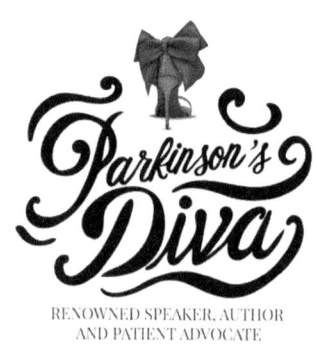

RENOWNED SPEAKER, AUTHOR
AND PATIENT ADVOCATE

PREFACE

"You will be secure, because there is hope; you will look about and take your rest in safety."

— Job 11:18

The purpose of this book is to share my life, faith, and journey from migrant to Parkinson's specialist, patient, caregiver, and ultimately, the Parkinson's Diva. This world seems to have lost its direction and purpose with many walking aimlessly not knowing where or whom to turn to for help, especially when confronted with a life altering diagnosis or experiencing a loss.

My journey to bring comfort and hope to others began as I sat at the bedside of a patient dying in pain and full of fear and regret about her life, I felt a deep sadness. I felt helpless as I tried to minister to her in her final hours so that her soul would be at peace. I often think about her and pray she found God's mercy. She had lived with Parkinson's disease for more than twenty years and had not only felt the loss of her body betraying her but also the loss of important relationships, someone to comfort or stay with her until she passed to the other side, crucial at times like this. I felt completely ill-prepared to help this woman cross to the other side. I stood there for a long time with eyes swollen with tears just watching as her frail and contorted body lay there lifeless.

I thought, *It can't all end like this for her.* She had lost hope and faith many moons ago. To this day, I carry the weight of remorse and guilt for not being able to counsel her spiritually and provide a peaceful send off. With the chaplain unavailable, I sat there holding her hand until the end came. As I sat there, I thought how ill-prepared we as physicians are to tend to the salient needs of the infirmed.

I promised myself then and there that I would start taking care of people holistically, body and soul. As Plato and many other great teachers and philosophers including Jesus have suggested throughout history, based on the fundamental premise that the soul, also known as psyche by some, is not only intricately intertwined with the body but more importantly — unlike the physical body — is imperishable. Thus, we should pay more attention to our spiritual condition. As Jesus demonstrated in the story of the ten lepers, healing comes from within (Luke 17:12-19). Other Greek philosophers had made similar observations, but their teaching has not influenced the world in the same manner. From the story of the ten lepers who encountered Jesus and asked for mercy (NIV version):

> [12] *As he was going into a village, ten men who had leprosy[a] met him. They stood at a distance* [13] *and called out in a loud voice, "Jesus, Master, have pity on us!"*
>
> [14] *When he saw them, he said, "Go, show yourselves to the priests." And as they went, they were cleansed.*
>
> [15] *One of them, when he saw he was healed, came back, praising God in a loud voice.* [16] *He threw himself at Jesus' feet and thanked him—and he was a Samaritan.*
>
> [17] *Jesus asked, "Were not all ten cleansed? Where are the other nine?* [18] *Has no one returned to give praise to God except this foreigner?"* [19] *Then he said to him, "Rise and go; your faith has made you well."*

Thus, as physicians, we should not only focus on the body or forget what sets us apart from other animals — our soul. Death comes to all of us at some point in life returning us to a spiritual state. This message of hope and courage to understand that true healing begins from the inside out has been my mission, and it is finally being put to words.

But *hope*? What exactly is it? And is it essential to have? Webster's

Dictionary defines hope: *"to desire with expectation of fulfillment."* It is not just a wish or a dream. It is an intrinsic belief that something we hope for will become a reality in the future. We may be able to live several weeks without food, days without water, minutes without oxygen, but not one second without *hope*.

If you are just commencing your journey with Parkinson's disease or any other stronghold in your life and have no idea what to do next or have been dancing with chronic illness as long as I have, then you have come to the right place. Some of you may feel like you are totally in the dark, trying to find a ray of hope to help guide your way. You have been in the abyss too long and are not sure if there is even light outside anymore. Let me tell you there is! You must continue moving forward.

As you find yourself plagued by an unwelcome disease like the oysters facing an unwanted intruder, you, too, can learn to transform your afflictions into something beautiful that will serve to beautify and give hope to others. In the process, you, too, will be transformed into something more beautiful and stronger than you ever imagined. I know because after years of being pressed, crushed, battling many illnesses, overcoming setbacks, feeling abandoned at times and in the dark, I have come to appreciate the marvels and mysteries of the depths. It is in the depths that one begins to have a better understanding of the spiritual realm. It is in this area that I have found great satisfaction realizing the value of taking time to know and explore the depths of faith. "Now faith is confidence in what we hope for and assurance for what we do not see" (Hebrews 11:1). If my struggles and suffering give someone else the courage to face their shortcomings due to illness with confidence and assurance for a better tomorrow, both physically and ultimately spiritually (after all we are spiritual beings dwelling temporarily in a shell made of flesh and bone), then my mission would be fulfilled.

I AM!

I am . . .
From the land of coal mines
Land of Pancho Villa
And women warrior's
where I grew up dreaming and learned to fly thanks to the
    love of my grandfather and the confidence he instilled in
    me
to become the woman, I am today
I AM! Two powerful words that attest of who I was, am,
    and will be
My story, my strußggles, my dreams, and my achievements
My present, my past and my future are all intertwined in
    two words
I am . . .
I am descendant of a family who loves friends, good food
    and a good conversation
I am Don Pedro's granddaughter lover of
Music and poetry and of Doña María artisan and matriarch
    of the faith
I am the apple of their eye
The one who learned not to fear anything because she
    knows who her God is –
the Master of the Universe
I am from the big house on Zaragoza Street built by my
grandfather with a fireplace made of volcanic rocks and
    marble
where the laughter and the
the fire of the hearth illuminated the home always

I am of two cultures of the North and South, Mexican, and
    American with boundless horizons
with roots as big as the oak tree
fragrant like the flower of magnolia and gardenia
as fragile as the velvety red tulip

I am . . .
Yet I am BOLD like a lioness
in tribute to my name

INTRODUCTION

Currently, we are living in uncertain times with tension brewing all around. No wonder anxiety, depression, and insomnia are on the rise. Young people, particularly, seem lost and untethered, walking in an emotional, mental, and physical state of exhaustion, continuously being bombarded by social media and in pursuit of the next big thing that promises immediate gratification. This inability to detach and disconnect and take time to reflect on what is important for our lives is swept under the rug, so society continues to become sicker and unhappier than ever before. We have forgotten that we are spiritual beings, meant to have a connection to a higher power from whom our strength emanates. Also, that we are created to live in companionship rather than alone. Yet, especially after the pandemic, we have become more isolated. I firmly believe it is this decline in social connectivity that is leading us to an increase in dementia.

While observing a budding neuron under Electronic Microscopy (EM), a scientist recording this event noted that the neuron attempted to make connections with another neuron by extending its dendrites (little arms). The attempt continued for four hours until this was achieved—only then did the dendrites cease moving about in search of another neuron to connect with. So, if even our brain, at its basic anatomical level, needs to have connections, why would we think that as complex beings, we would do okay being isolated?

An extensive Harvard-sponsored study conducted on the cause of happiness, which was begun in the early part of last century, determined that it's not the money, status, job, education, power, or influence that makes us happy but rather the social connections one has. Other mammals of higher intelligence like whales also become sad and die when taken away from their pods.

The other cause that has shown to improve health is having faith and believing in a higher power. Scientists have shown that involvement in religious and spiritual practices is associated with improved health outcomes, including longevity, coping skills, and quality of life—including during terminal illness.

So why are we not prescribing religion and spirituality? Both give us a cultural construct to our behaviors, value systems, and experiences, which will help us (1) stay healthy; (2) deal with chronic illnesses in a positive way; and (3) give us a rewarding and fuller life.

I love the story of Job. Lately, my faith has been questioned by people from whom I would not expect such insensitive remarks. It was said that perhaps my continued physical decline over the last two years was due to my lack of faith and prayer. This struck a chord, bringing me right back to the Book of Job. I wonder if my reaction was like that of Job's. First, I was taken aback by the insinuation that my ailments are caused by my lack of faith or poor relation with God. I asked how could they ask this question?

How could they know the extent of deep my faith?

They said like Job's friends did, "It is because you are not getting better."

"Well, perhaps God knows why," I responded.

All I know is that I live daily by His grace alone and from Job and many others in the Bible I have learned to take each day as it comes.

Now more than ever, this story continues to fascinate me because, despite all the personal losses, he remained steadfast in his belief in his ONE true God. Not an easy feat, especially when you find yourself standing alone against the world. Job found the courage to ask to speak to God, the creator and have a heart-to-heart talk and ask *why?* I know that as I found myself increasingly troubled and plagued by disease, I, too, became angry initially. As a Christian, I thought I was offending God by being angry or questioning His love for me or His plans for my life. But remembering the story of a homeless, penniless, friendless, isolated, and covered in painful sores man, I, too, was afraid of expressing my true sentiments of anger, despair, frustration, and reproaching God for my misfortune. Slowly I began to realize that God, like a parent, is delighted in His children coming to Him with their struggles and is always eager to help. However, just like any parent would do, the aid (guidance) given is dependent on the lesson He wants us to learn, or trait

He wants to mold in us. Further, I discovered that expressing these feelings was not only cathartic but also helped me understand my own limitations and strengths. But it also has helped me build my faith and understand there are some things that must remain a conundrum.

I loved embroidering, especially on cool breezy afternoons sitting on my grandma's porch with her and my mom. We would pass the time talking, sharing stories, and laughing. I used to get a lot of comments about all the knots on the back of whatever I was working on. Grandma would say it does not matter much because what matters is the finished product when you look at it right side up. So even if it looks like a total mess on close inspection from the wrong side, when it's finished, you will be able to appreciate a beautiful work of art. This is what our life and daily struggles look like up close; but to God, who is interested in the final product, He appreciates that to create a beautiful tapestry, you may have to make a mess at first. I want to remind everyone that we all have hidden potential living inside, and unless we are put to the fiery test (like Job was), it will continue to lay dormant, being of no use to anyone. Thus, sometimes we experience loss and disease as a catalyst to turn us into a medium through which others will not only simply survive but grow and flourish.

Our trials at times may feel as if fire was being sent to us from heaven to punish us. However, not all adversities are meant to destroy us and some in fact make us stronger and give birth to something we never knew we possessed inside. For instance, we always feel bad when forest fires occur, and we mourn for the loss of the trees that get burnt, as is natural. But what we fail to see is that the only way new life in the forest can take place is through these events. I would have never discovered my true self and learned from my weaknesses and strengths to grow had I not received a young onset of Parkinson's (YOPD) diagnosis. In the grand forests of California and Yellowstone Park, when all the regular pinecones are destroyed by the fire, the lodgepole pinecone not only resists this intense heat without perishing, but within it, holds the key to new life and reforestation. After everything else has been ravaged by fire, this cone finally releases its seed to allow life to begin anew. So, press on through your fiery storms because trying to avoid these tests is like trying to avoid living, and without goals to strive for, one simply stops growing. But more importantly we no longer have a thriving vibrant and abundant life.

Faith, like fear and uncertainty, are invisible forces which require a form of acceptance and belief. Where will you spend your energy and on what will you build your future? The choice is yours.

CHAPTER 1

Road of Life

*"A person often meets his destiny on the road he took
to avoid it."*

— Jean de La Fontaine

his has certainly been the case for me. It's strange to think about, but many people around the globe know the Parkinson's Diva. Although few know the woman behind the moniker. Even fewer know that that my work for the Parkinson's community was a calling from God. My life's journey became the foundation for the name.

Many of my high school friends wanted to be doctors and participated in medical clubs, not me. Honestly, the only thing I knew for certain was that I had a knack for languages. I even considered working as a UN interpreter early on in my career. I was especially shy during my early high school years since English was my second language. Having been ridiculed often when I first came to the States, I felt very insecure about public speaking. Boy, has that changed. Once I gave a lecture to an audience of 10,000 people without batting an eye. Anyway, I have always been fascinated by the workings of the brain and the mind particularly in the interplay of the psyche and the structural parts of the brain. My father was a family doctor in Mexico and my mom a nurse; they had high expectations of me becoming a physician. I had absolutely no intention whatsoever of being a doctor. As a senior, I applied to Yale as an early admission. Not really knowing what I would major in, I knew I was heading north to an Ivy League school. I thought some sort of science would be likely, because of my inquisitive nature.

For whatever reason, on the last day before the holidays, I found myself wandering about the halls of my high school. As I passed by the office, something pulled me in. There I encountered an extremely pleasant young Hispanic woman. Being a social butterfly, I immediately struck up a conversation. It became my destiny.

It turns out that she was from my hometown, so I stayed longer talking to her than I had intended. Plus, we had the same name, which is not unusual—Maria is a very common name. Nevertheless, it felt as if we had a deeper connection. She was a recruiter for another Ivy League school. She asked if I had applied and I told her I made an early decision elsewhere. She began telling me about a hot new degree program this university had just opened, interconnecting several fields of study, which caught my attention immediately. Seeing my enthusiasm, she said I should apply. I didn't think this was feasible since I had already accepted admission elsewhere. Being that the deadline for early admission was that day, she insisted I fill out the application on the spot. I figured I had nothing to lose, so I did. Within a week, I was accepted, and the course of my life was altered forever.

People, like flowers, bloom in their own time and follow their own journeys. To succeed in taking the correct road in life, we must focus on our own individual gifts and talents. We must first begin by being kind to ourselves, accepting our strengths and flaws. Cultivate a heart full of gratitude. Use your uniqueness to find your passion to better yourself and others.

CHAPTER 2

The Queen "B"

(Because of my nickname, Bebzie.)

"... And who knows but that you have come to your
royal position for such a time as this?"
— Esther 4:14

Before I was a *Diva*, I was a princess to my grandfather, who doted on me from the day I was born, partly because I was the first and only grandchild for many years. Secondly, because I was born a special needs child, this garnered me a special place in my grandfather's heart, so much so that when he developed dementia, I was the only one he remembered without fail. Thanks to his love and constant teachings, I can say I am the person that I am today: outspoken, confident, and a believer.

Growing up, I loved my grandfather's cologne. I would keep his handkerchiefs and scarves because I loved the scent of him. To this day, I get emotional each time I smell Old Spice. He also fostered my love of reading and knowledge, buying me every book and encyclopedia from one particular traveling salesman, just like the movie *Secondhand Lions*. Fortunately, the salesman did not have a lion or a plane—because I am certain we would have ended up with those as well. My grandfather was a combination of Michael Cain and Robert Duvall, full of stories and advice for the youth. His home was a fun place for a child to grow up, very lively, to say the least.

But I enjoyed many privileges my siblings and other cousins never had, like staying up late watching movies, sleeping undisturbed in the morning with all the fans pointed in my direction, which drove everyone insane. Sometimes, while everyone slept, I would go to the roof in the middle of the night to catch a breeze and watch the stars. Even to this day, I'm still in awe as I gaze at the heavens. My grandmother had a telescope and loved to study the planets. On a few occasions, we were lucky enough to witness shooting stars, a rare comet whose name I can't recall, and at least once, we saw an alignment of several planets. I have always been fascinated with the stars, but not enough to leave the ground where I stand, more in a theoretical sense. It is interesting to me that since ancient times, man predicted events based on the stars and created calendars that lasted centuries. But more fascinating to me is the fact that each Maria in our family, spanning four generations, was born during an equinox or a solstice, which I think makes us pretty special.

During my pre-teenage years, Dad and I were very close. He loved for me to sing with him at all the parties, and if you are Hispanic, there are always a lot of parties! We celebrate everything! One special day I remember, in particular, was the day I won the school pageant when I was nine years old, thanks to my father's love.

In Mexico, as in many places, the contests are based not only on popularity but also on funds raised. I knew I had no chance of winning because we did not have much money, and I was running against the daughter of a wealthy businessman. But I did not let this dissuade me from dreaming of being queen for a day. I sold everything I could find under the sun, even borrowed the stove at the elementary school, and with help from my friends, made 200 burgers to sell at recess. Yet, when the day arrived to tally the votes for Miss Congeniality, I had no problem beating some of the other contestants. However, rising to the top as whisked cream was going to take some doing.

Apparently, Dad had a plan up his sleeves, and he did not share it with me or anyone else. Three separate times during the evening, the money was counted and added to the grand total. Dad, unbeknownst to me, dispensed a little at a time and saved the rest of the money to be placed in my ballot box at the last second when everyone else's money had been counted. Watching the evening tallies place me lower and lower in the running, I was sure I would be the last person in the court. I looked over at my dad as he intently watched the board with a poker face.

Summoning me with his finger, he said, "Go put this envelope in the box and hurry before they take it up." I did as he said. However, I was certain there was no way I could land first place, but if I were lucky, I could land in third place. With a big sigh and a shoulder shrug, I placed the envelope in the collection box and walked toward the entrance where my dad was watching. When I reached the doorway, he pulled me in close and whispered, "Let's wait a second and see what happens, then we can go home."

"Sure, Dad," I said, trying to force a smile. It was nearly nine o'clock in the evening, and we had been there for hours. The excitement of possibly winning was beginning to fade and fatigue was kicking in. Dad must have been exhausted, too, since we had come to the school as soon as he got home from work and neither one of us had eaten. Standing there leaning on Dad, waiting for the total tally, my eyes started closing. Then I heard a man's voice over the loudspeaker.

"Maria Luisa De León from Mrs. Calderon's third-grade class is the new *Adelita*." *Adelita* was the endearing name given to Pancho Villa's female companion. She is considered to be a heroine of the Republic, particularly for those of us who lived in the northern part of Mexico. She was said to be both gentle and fierce. I could not believe my ears. I turned to Dad for affirmation, and his wide grin confirmed what I had just heard.

"Oh my God! I can't believe it!" I could not stop yelling, jumping up and down, and smiling like a fool. "Dad, did you do this? But how?"

"I could not let anyone outshine my daughter! You will be the prettiest and smartest *Adelita* ever! Now let's go get a burger; you must be starving."

"Dad, how did you pull it off?" I repeatedly asked throughout dinner, but he never said a word—he just smiled. Of course, as a child, I did not appreciate my father's grand gesture of love as I do now. I feel my eyes tear up as I recount this story and miss him dearly since he has passed away. Even more touched I became, when years later, I discovered that he had taken out all his savings just to see his daughter happy—his selfless love for me was loud and clear. Some may think that it was foolish of him to do this, since we were struggling financially. Yet, his gesture speaks volumes for the type of man he was and the love he had for me and his family. When he passed away, I found a picture of us tucked into his duct-taped wallet, which I had given to him as a joke since he thought duct tape was the answer to everything. He loved to show his wallet to everyone and tell them that his daughter, the doctor, had given it to him, which always made me chuckle.

The day before the November 20th, known as "el *Día de la Revolución*" (Revolution Day), Dad was ready at first light with a truck he borrowed and an entire crew to decorate my float for the parade. I was the errand girl tasked with going to the store to buy decorating supplies and candy, of course. My eyes lit up as my name was spelled in big letters on top of the float for everyone to see. There must have been a million pictures taken of me that day. Being my grandfather's favorite granddaughter, he insisted on purchasing every picture. Having so many picture albums of me, while my siblings shared an album which was not even full, did not help with their perception of me as a queen.

My brother jokes that until he was a grownup, he did not know that watermelons were supposed to be red because he always got the rind. He is the jokester of the family and loves to embellish childhood memories. This is all in jest—he and I are extremely close. Being so much older than him, when I returned home for the holidays after my first semester of college, he would not leave my side.

If you were to listen to my siblings, you would think I grew up with a silver spoon in my mouth. My brother claims he was forced to work in the hot sun from dusk to dawn with only bread and water while I got to lounge around reading in whatever the coolest place in the house was. In a way, this was true because I have always been extremely sensitive to the heat and had so many allergies, plus the fact that melanoma runs in our family, and my grandfather never wanted me exposed to the sun.

He also indulged my and my grandmother's love for books. She and I usually spent *siesta* time reading while he worked and everyone else took a nap. He would purchase a new book for me and a western novel for my grandma weekly. Both my grandma and I had the status of queen as my grandpa loved and dotted on us both. We did have the reign of the house, especially since due to all the immigration status of my family traveling back and forth to the States I always remained with my grandparents. Thus, I feel in some way they were the ones who raised me. Even after I moved to Texas permanently, I continued to spend every summer and holiday with them until I was twenty-three, when my academic responsibilities no longer allowed me the time.

Of course, my brother, whom I love dearly, loves to poke fun at me all the time, regaling everyone with incredible tales of "Your Royal Highness." I think it is hysterical, but deep down, I do love tiaras and holding court! One of my favorite stories of his is recounting why he likes to eat lemon-flavored *paletas* (Mexican lemon ice pops) to this day. He claims to never have tasted or seen any other flavors because of me. I was always the one who went with grandpa to buy them because my brother and sister, who are much younger, usually were playing somewhere or swimming in grandpa's water tank. I would get about 15-20 *paletas* each time in all types of flavors, and when we got home everyone would choose their own. Of course, I always tried something new and exotic each time, like mango or my two favorites: guava and pineapple. Grandma was the same; she liked trying new things. There were five of us, but sometimes our other cousins would come over, and I suppose, since he never liked to get out of the water tank, he always had last pickings, always ending up with same flavor. Secretly, I think lemon is his favorite. But he loves to give me grief. He still chooses lemon flavor whenever we go to the Mexican *paleteria* (ice pop store) in Houston. Any time they open a new Mexican candy store, bakery or *paleteria*, he insists on taking me there right away. We sit there and reminisce and laugh a lot.

Back in Mexico, the summers were brutally hot as there were no air conditioners, water always ran out in the middle of the day for several hours, and everything was closed from two to six o'clock. All one could do was try to nap or sit quietly somewhere in a cool area of the house. If we were lucky, we could catch a breeze from one of those recurrent summer hailstorms. Because it was so unbearably hot, showering only made things worse. But as I said there was never any running water in the afternoons so anytime the opportunity presented itself, I would always volunteer to go with my grandfather to work. There were lots of perks. First was spending time with grandpa, but second, he took me to cool places and bought me cold drinks and snow cones. Plus, I usually got a new novel or magazine to read.

My neighbor, who was my dearest friend, usually came along on most trips with grandpa. We always had a blast, she and I. Although she was five years older, we were inseparable. She was either at my grandpa's house, or I at hers. I preferred going to her house because they had a window air conditioner, so we would play Uno at her house for hours. On our last adventure together, we decided to go to Acapulco. While there the Miss Mexico pageant was taking place, so my friend suggested I should compete the following year. I thought she was funny. Back then, I was not confident in my looks or skills or even bold enough to do such a thing. These days, if I had the chance, I would try it in a heartbeat.

So that was the extent of my involvement in pageantry until I entered a Bible pageant for all Southern Baptist churches of Houston, where I was bombarded with questions about scripture for several hours. It felt more like an interrogation as I remained in the spotlight, staring into darkness, while the judges spewed out their questions in a manner akin to that of Charlie Brown's teacher's voice *wawawawa*. I won first place. This was truly the first time I received a crown. When I was crowned *Adelita*, I wore a typical charro hat.

One way I have learned to feel empowered and empower other women, whether they are dealing with trauma, loss, or chronic illness, is to walk tall like you and I are wearing a crown. As if you were next in line to the throne because you are the daughter of the king. When you learn to trust in a higher power you will begin to see situations from different angles. You will realize that circumstances cannot hold you because your future is secure. The present situation may not change, but a positive attitude will make all the difference. Learn to walk looking up and forward rather than down and back. Get excited for the future. Remember, you are in control of it. As one of my favorite authors, Isabel Allende, once wrote: "You are the storyteller of your own life." It is up to you to decide how that story is going to change you and the world. I come from a long line of storytellers, and I want the craziness, the trials, and the victories of my life to make us go *wow*, laugh, cry, and perhaps learn something valuable that can be passed on to others.

Recall that serene moment when the world went completely black for a fleeting moment during the last solar eclipse. As the darkness grew, there was an awe accompanied by a deafening sound, reminding us just how small and insignificant we are in the grand scheme of the universe and how fragile our lives are. Yet, against all the odds, here we stand capable of flourishing even in the midst of darkness, getting stronger and more resilient like a piece of coal as it transforms into a magnificent, brilliant diamond. Now . . . straighten your crown and walk like the queen that you are meant to be.

CHAPTER 3

The Royal Couch

"What on earth could be more luxurious than a sofa,
a book, and a cup of coffee? . . .

Was ever anything so civil?"

— Anthony Trollope

Now that I am a married woman with so many illnesses, I spend a great deal of time reclining on my favorite chaise lounge, lovingly nicknamed the Queen Cleopatra sofa or in my case the sofa of the Queen B by my husband. Because I spend an enormous amount of time on it, he jokingly suggests that I should be transported like a queen on my throne wherever I go. The chaise is so much part of me that my husband also teases me that I should have *boyees*—the people known to carry the chair, also known as *Palaquins*—with me at all times. Although . . . there was one time I wished I had my own portable chaise . . .

I had just undergone back surgery and decided to attend a writers' convention for physicians near Boston. Not sure what I was thinking, choosing to travel a long distance, then attend an event where I would be forced to sit for several hours, but that's just who I am. My husband has said that the only thing predictable about me is my unpredictability. Once we arrived at Cape Cod, I was thrilled to meet one of my favorite authors, Tess Gerritsen, bestselling novelist and creator of the *Rizzoli & Isles* series. As the evening went on, I struggled to remain sitting from the pain. But I did not want to leave the conference, since I too, had visions of becoming a bestselling author someday.

The next day, as I stumbled into the conference room, stooped over and hobbling from the surgical pain and the Parkinson's to boot, I was struck by an unusual sight. As I entered the conference room looking for a strategic place to call my own, I stumbled upon a woman lying in a hospital bed smack in the middle of the room. I couldn't help but think to myself, why did I not think of that? My chaise would not look so out of place, and I probably would not even be noticed. Oh well, *c'est la vie*! I would never have such audacity to ask for a bed or sofa to be brought to a conference room for me, but I can always cite that the event set a precedent should I ever need one.

The woman who had occupied the bed in the morning disappeared after lunch for several hours, probably doing what I should have been doing — sleeping, resting, and taking my pain pills. As my pain kept creeping higher the longer the conference ran, I began looking out for the woman, trying to decide if I should pull a *coup*. Although my solstice birth says people born during this time tend to be bold, in the end I was too afraid I'd embarrass myself and endured the discomfort for as long as I could before calling it quits. Sometimes I wish I could be carried around as I imagine Cleopatra had been, making a grand entrance and not having to look for a seat close to the exit or near the bathroom or with enough room to prop up my legs. Once I was frantically looking for elevators at Chicago's O'Hare airport because the escalators were broken, racing to a connecting flight, short of breath and wheezing due to pain, while desperately trying to find a wheelchair attendant. But alas, one was not to be found.

I was on the verge of tears and nearly experienced a head injury. Sweating like a mad woman, short of breath, my medications completely worn off, and no time to take it again. I was running, my legs felt like molasses and heavy as cement. I struggled to pull myself up the stairs with my upper body as my lower body was useless. I almost reached the top and slipped. I imagined myself like one of those cartoons, slithering all the way to the bottom in a melted puddle. I gripped the rail and literally crawled up the last five steps to a post at the top of the escalator which helped me regain my posture as much as I could. I had no strength left in me to move another inch. I was certain I was going to miss my connecting flight home, but as I looked up, my gate was right in front of me. After a quick glance around, I saw there was no place to sit, and afraid of falling, I stood holding the post until boarding began.

In fact, as I convalesced from one of my many surgeries, alone at home, pondering my plight and how I was NOT going to let Parkinson's or any other illness dictate how I was to live my life, the idea of the Parkinson's Diva began to take shape on this very couch.

Over the years, even when convalescing from an exacerbation of my many illnesses or recovering from one of my many surgeries and forced to be bedbound, it has helped me stay in the center of the family get-togethers during holidays, birthdays, and other special events. The children, my daughter, nephew, and nieces all grew up spending time around my couch playing all sorts of games, sharing stories, watching movies, and singing songs. My nephew and daughter would take turns crafting silly hairdos on me and making up funny songs and videos with me and about me. My sofa is near the fireplace, my favorite spot in the house, just as it was in my grandparents' home.

For many years, this well-crafted piece of furniture has witnessed countless moments of joy, tears, rage, frustration, desperation, hopelessness, and each time seeing me reemerge stronger and more determined. I think my husband had it right calling my sofa "the Queen B couch."

From this couch, I saw my daughter along with my nephew and nieces grow into dedicated, passionate, caring, and loving young individuals. One is getting a nursing degree; another is a geneticist working on important diseases like familial hypertension and rare neurological diseases. And my daughter is getting a masters in toxicology. With scientists and scholars like these young people leading the next generation, I am certain we will make headway in helping to care for and treat people living with these infirmities—and perhaps, dare I dream, to unlock the main environmental cause leading to the increase in Parkinson's globally.

Although they may never be able to step in my shoes or walk where I have walked among the infirmed, they have felt the impact of the many stories told around the fireplace sitting on my couch. The echoes and vibrations of the sounds of victory and struggle from those who have shaped my life have helped these youngsters build empathy and love for those around them. These days, I sit on my royal couch, proud, thinking that perhaps a bit of me goes with them in their own life journey—not in my shoes but on the same soil beneath their feet.

CHAPTER 4

Stilettos

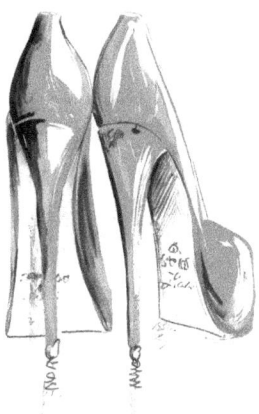

Shoe Love is True Love

An icon of hope for women around the globe with Parkinson's.

M argie, whose mother had suffered from Parkinson's and had been a patient of mine, called to check up on me and ask how I was doing. I responded that I was chillin' on my sofa wearing the one and only pair of high heels I had kept. My favorite Kate Spade three-inch, pink wedges in the shape of a car (a picture of me holding one of the shoes is featured in the women's booklet: *In Her Shoes*.) But even as I try to put them on, I fail to keep my balance, immediately falling forward. However, I keep them as a reminder of the fashionista that I am, as well as to never forget that, first and foremost, I am a woman . . . a mom, a wife, a daughter, and a friend.

One of the initial symptoms of my Parkinson's was foot dystonia.

Dystonia in this case focal because initially localized to my foot is an involuntary sustained contraction of the muscles twisting and contorting my foot. It began in my left foot, causing severe pain and discomfort when attempting to introduce my foot into the shoe. Initially, I fell several times because I was used to putting on my shoes standing up and the pain along with the loss of balance from my foot contorting caused me to fall each time. Forget about wearing boots. Due to the increasing severity of pain and risk of falling, I slowly began to get rid of my extensive shoe collection, one pair at a time. What remained was a single bland and unappealing pair of tennis shoes. I refused to part with the pink wedges, even if I could no longer wear them.

People often say that clothes make the man; in my case, I truly believe that shoes make the woman. In fact, one of my favorite quotes is one by Marylin Monroe, a great diva herself. "Give a woman the right pair of shoes and she can conquer the world." Funny, because my daughter has never been a believer of this until recently. As she was packing her things to move away from home, she came and showed me her extensive collection of shoes. She said, "Mom, you were right about the shoes! Now that I am becoming more like you, I have a growing collection of shoes." Looking at how proud she was of her shoes, I simply smiled. There are some things that are intrinsic and can't be avoided. Even as a child, she always gravitated to the most beautiful fancy stilettos and told me I would look good in them. She had impeccable taste even then, just like her grandma, great grandma, and mother.

I was described by my patients and peers as a stylish neurologist, often because of my footwear. At the young age of three, back in Mexico, I would walk around all day in my mom's three- to four-inch heels, wearing a ballerina outfit or a dress, along with my grandmother's double-loop string of pearls. During my school years in Mexico, I was in every dance the school put on. I simply loved wearing all those colorful costumes. With the dress and costume collection my grandma kept from mother's school years, there were enough clothes for me and several of my girlfriends who shared my passion for singing and entertaining to dress up and put on a weekly variety show. We would do this in my grandma's backyard where there was a stage built by my grandfather, a remnant of a previous room in the house. We loved putting on shows for the whole neighborhood. Of course, I was typically the main star, imitating many of the popular female singers of the time. We put on performances for several years and always had a good gathering who cheered us on.

The town I grew up in was a small, unpaved community with no reliable ground transportation, so we walked everywhere through streets full of rocks, pebbles, and boulders. My mother loved to walk in high heels all throughout the town carrying my brother. (I certainly do not know how she did this because, even as a baby, he weighed ten pounds.) In her youth, grandma did the same, so I suppose it was natural for me to want to wear heels. If you were unfortunate to fall, among the rocky terrain you were certain to get a second-degree burn due to the extreme hot weather. Even though I was very clumsy with weak ankles and fell all the time due to my birth problems, this never stopped me from wearing high heels. First only at home then outside as I got older. So, I became a pro at walking in high heels on uneven terrain, and I continued to wear them, even as I attended college in Philadelphia.

Walking on ice with pointy black satin heels is not exactly the smartest thing to do; yet for the first winter in Philly, I walked all over campus, slipping and sliding and enduring more than one fall. It is funny how being young has a way of masking any injuries, so despite the many falls, I was no worse for wear except for a few humorous and embarrassing moments. I paraded around in such fancy shoes and walked city blocks in them without a care. You take so many things for granted when you are healthy and young until you can no longer simply walk on snow without falling and tumbling all over the place.

It had been years since I left the northeast to settle back in Texas. My Parkinson's had been under control for several years, and I returned to Boston for a conference. It was, as I remember, breathtaking, quiet, and pristine after a fresh snowfall. I took it all in when I arrived. However, the next morning was an entirely different matter. A nasty layer of ice had formed, making all the sidewalks very slick and slippery. Although I don't use or require assistive devices, my balance is not good, and I experienced tremendous difficulty just walking the short distance to the conference across the street. I used to walk over piles of snow without a thought during my medical school years and now a small hill was obstructing my way, and I was stuck. It was too far to go to the next intersection, and as I tried to cross over on what I thought was the most solid of choices, I slipped on the ice and fell backward into the frozen water, soaking my behind. With tears at the edge of my eyes, I thought I would go in, get something to warm me up, then try going back to my hotel to change clothes before my talk in the afternoon.

As I walked into the conference hall, one of the coordinators caught me and said there had been a change and wanted me to present first. *But, but . . .* The words just rattled in my head. My back was hurting, my mouth was dry, and not to mention the icy shiver beginning to run through me because my entire *derriere* was frozen wet. Needless to say, my presentation was less than stellar. This is what living with Parkinson's is like. One day you are a great orator, and the next you can't even get a thought out or form a complete sentence due to severe dry mouth and dreading the embarrassment, should I appear a fool in front of Harvard's prestigious academicians. With dripping wet pants, to boot! So, in the end, my contributions were noted, and my contributions had a positive impact on the project. As for my plans to walk around Harvard, that was a different story. I had never felt so clumsy, unstable, and old.

I wondered if others have as much difficulty as I have experienced living with Parkinson's. I always loved shoes because I felt they could take me places. Now it takes some doing to find the right shoes. Buying shoes is a lot like Goldilocks's ordeal. They can't be too slippery or have too much traction because they will cause me to tumble and fall. They certainly can't be too high. No more stilettos! What I would give to prance around in one of those dainty pairs of shoes again. Even my mom, who is well into her seventies, can still wear those three-inch heels making me quite jealous. Nothing makes a pair of legs look more stunning than a beautiful high heel in my opinion. Forget using shoes with straps and buckles. These are quite difficult to buckle or tie especially if you have tremors, dystonia, and loss of fine motor movement. Although I tend to wear a lot of slip-on shoes a size bigger so I can slide them on easier, I do not stop searching for the most functional yet attractive and feminine shoes out there.

I recall the very first time my grandfather took me shoe shopping. I picked out the prettiest red shoes in the store. I was supposed to go buy a pair of black shoes to go with my school uniform. Mom was not happy, and per her request, Grandpa was to take me back to buy black oxford shoes. As he noticed my sadness, he whispered in my ear, "Don't worry, you can keep the red ones, too." My spirits were immediately lifted, and off we went.

I have become quite the shoe maven with years of experience in all types of terrain, climate, budget, and lifestyle. With the onset of Parkinson's disease (PD) and the loss of my prized collection, often a topic of conversation among my staff and patients, for the first time, I felt at a loss. Even though during the pandemic I did not wear shoes for nearly two years, I am happy to report that I am now building a new collection of even more interesting shoes (*wink, wink*). Finding a beautiful pair of shoes I can wear without tripping, falling, or spending an hour just to put on or buckle is like finding a rare gem.

Shortly after the symptoms of dystonia in my foot began, I found myself wearing sneakers for the first time since middle school. It was mandatory to wear them to gym class, but I absolutely hated them for years because they were simply not very attractive. Plus, they always seemed to cause me knee pain each time I tried to wear them during my formative years and again while working at the hospital.

During the first few years of my journey as a patient with Parkinson's despite my training and knowledge, life was a lot more challenging and complex than I had anticipated it to be for a person living with PD. No matter what stage in life you may find yourself in, no one ever wants a diagnosis of a chronic illness, much less a progressive neurodegenerative disease. I was in the midst of building a new office with a thriving practice and was raising a toddler. My grandmother, who had practically raised me, had just passed away from complications of a brain tumor and Parkinson's. I was still recovering from the loss of both grandparents and the physical and emotional strain caregiving had put on me and my family and marriage for a year. Now, less than a year after her passing, just as I thought I would get control of my life again, I began to notice the symptoms of a familiar friend. Totally unprepared was I for this close friend to suddenly move in permanently, uprooting my entire operation as a mom, wife, and physician. In an instant, my life was upside down once more.

One would think that having treated hundreds of patients with PD, it would be so much easier to recognize. We all know the saying that doctors are the worst patients. We never follow the rules, and my case was proving just that. My presentation of PD was not following the so-called rules of typical Parkinson's. I was a young, thirtysomething woman with atypical features, not recognized at the time as being a premotor and early manifestation of a common neurological disease. Sometimes doctors are prone to get the most bizarre and rare illnesses or otherwise unconventional presentations of common diseases. I suppose this is God's way of keeping us humble and teaching us compassion and empathy toward human suffering. As my grandparents' doctor and caregiver, I learned a lot about showing compassion and kindness to those suffering.

But as I quickly learned, having the knowledge does not always translate to achieving a fast diagnosis or finding the proper treatment on the first try. This was my case. It took three years for someone to concur with the notion that I indeed had early onset Parkinson's disease. The assurance made me ecstatic at first until I began to contend with the side effects of the medications. The same meds I had prescribed to my grandmother and my patients hundreds of times, the same ones I trusted and felt extremely comfortable prescribing and manipulating to the advantage of patients, were now wreaking havoc on my person. The side effects seemed worse than the illness at the onset of my journey.

Seventeen years later, I have come full circle again contending with a barrage of side effects which make living and enjoying life that much more difficult. I often wonder what is worse: dealing with the symptoms of the disease or the unwanted side effects of the medications? My husband believes I should just stop all medications, so I won't suffer so much which on the surface sounds terrific. But the reality is that without the Parkinson's medications I would probably die a lot sooner. This disease has a way of impacting every aspect of your life and taking over ever so slowly that before you realize you stop being the person you once were before. If I were to stop the medications, I would stop being me all together. I am a completely different person; one I do not like. That person is dull and apathetic, irritable, with no spark of life, can't move well and has trouble swallowing, talking, and having any dreams or goals.

Even though I feel like I always have ten balls in the air trying to manage my symptoms and side effects I refuse to give in or stop fighting. So, I endure the pain and whatever other side effect of the myriad medications and slew of diseases I have without ever giving up on who I am—a dreamer, a fashionista, and a neurology geek. Although at times, I feel I have lost so much. For instance, I don't do half of the things I used to either because I am in a flare-up from one of my many chronic diseases, have no energy or simply find it too exhausting. My own mother told me recently, you are not the same woman you used to be. This made me sad, but it also made me want to fight harder for my daughter's sake so that I can be more present in her life. I once was the life of the party, now is hard to even get to the party. But when I do, I always have the right shoes and *beaucoup* stories to tell.

At the beginning of my diagnosis, I fell asleep at the wheel due to the dopamine agonist. Obviously, I had to stop taking them. Initially, the old levodopa formulations caused me to have severe orthostatic hypotension (low blood pressure) and nausea. This was extremely challenging and difficult to overcome since I was working full-time. Plus, I needed to be on call, *and* I had a child to raise. Then came the worst part: shortly after my PD diagnosis, I was diagnosed with metastatic thyroid cancer. The treatments compounded with PD left me unable to walk unaided. I began using a walker because of the weakness and heaviness of my legs. My legs felt like they were encased in cement.

Holding up my head was the next problem. I could barely lift it from my pillow without using my hands. Once out of bed, my head hung like a cherry on a stem. I remember going to Walmart because my daughter wanted something and literally slouching my body over the cart. My daughter pulled it forward from the front because I had no strength to push it. As I slouched, hanging on to the cart as if my life depended on it, my eyes were fixed on the ground. What I noticed next from the corner of my eye was a pair of royal blue satin stiletto heels. Admiring the beautiful shoes, I felt a bit jealous and sad because I was not certain at that moment how long it would take for me to walk like a normal person again, much less if I could wear such an exquisite pair of shoes.

Here I was, dragging my feet in less than attractive footwear at thirty-something years of age. The anguish became greater when I looked up to see an elegantly dressed woman probably in her seventies, dressed to a tee. Although, as I think about that incident, it seemed strange to see anyone dressed so elegantly to go grocery shopping. So, I imagined she had forgotten something on her way to a wedding party or perhaps she was an old socialite who is always completely dressed up to be ready for any occasion. As I continued to lay on my couch convalescing, contemplating my stilettos as I spoke to Margie on the phone, I told her that I was not about to have a seventy-year-old woman show me up. Because sadly, I knew of so many women with Parkinson's who stopped feeling feminine or doing things for themselves to feel good due to the disease. I told her that I did not want the disease to dictate my life so to complete the I still got it look, even though I have PD, I had bought a t-shirt that said, "I Make Parkinson's Look Sexy."

No sooner had we hung up the phone than she showed up at my door with a box full of feather boas, a tiara, lots of bling and additional treats, and my favorite book about a duck who runs for president. This was the inaugural Parkinson's Diva party which continued for several hours, until my daughter was dropped off from school by my friend (because I could not drive). My friend, her daughter and mine joined in the party, and by then, I had put on my special t-shirt and was wearing a tiara my friend had brought me. Because I had already started to write my first book on women issues and Parkinson's, my friends and later my husband thought I should call it *The Parkinson's Diva*, and the picture of me with the tiara became the portrait for the book.

They all agreed with me that every girl, no matter the age, should have a princess party at least once in their life. We spent an entire afternoon playing dress-up, being girls with no disease or care in the world. I thought the party would be our own little secret. That did not last since my husband found all the boa feathers in my vacuum cleaner. That afternoon brought back fond memories of similar festivities of unencumbered days as a young girl living in Mexico, involving a lot of confetti, lots of bling, fancy dresses, and high heels to celebrate the birthdays of my dolls.

Shoes will always have a special place in my heart because they remind me of the bond my grandfather and I forged, but more important is the spiritual significance they hold for me. There is a phrase that every journey begins with a single step. However, in life—to be victorious, happy, fulfilled, and abundant, even when confronted by trials and tribulations—one must begin with a single footstep of faith. Shoes symbolize restoration and reinstatement of status, for it was only the free who wore shoes; slaves went barefoot. Have you ever tried to run or walk barefooted on a scorching hot, uneven terrain full of rocks? It is extremely difficult to navigate or go far even, making some areas off limits, as I experienced many a times in my old country. Many injuries occurred as a result. Thus, shoes represent *readiness*. For a soldier to be able to run into battle, he must first put on his shoes. Shoes allow one to roam freely and provide traction.

This is also true within the spiritual realm. If we are to stand strong and unwavering against the difficulties and challenges that we as people experience on this earth such as trauma, loss, and chronic illnesses, we must first put on our armor of God, which according to Ephesians 6:15, begins with binding our feet with the preparation of the gospel of peace. These shoes of peace are the means through which we can support, persevere, and stand firm in our daily lives against oppression and adversity. Not only have my spiritual shoes improved through the years of dealing with multiple health issues but also my capacity to withstand the storms and the arrows flung at me from all directions as well. Remember, when I first went to college, being young, naïve, inexperienced, and broke, I did not have proper shoes, causing me a lot of falls and injuries . . . until I got snow boots. I would never have learned had I not experienced the difficulty of walking on ice with stiletto heels. Likewise, I would never have realized how strong and tenacious I could be had it not been for all the struggles I faced. However,

I have also learned that sometimes to feel real joy, you must go barefooted along the shore, risking injury or fall—or better yet, allowing God to carry us through the difficult portions of our life to not cause harm to ourselves.

CHAPTER 5

Livin' on a Prayer

We're all on a journey
With two paths to take
One that is right
And the one that can break
So together when sharing

Surely we'll find
it's the treasure of life
That can give peace of mind

— Excerpts from *The Treasure of Life*
by Olive Walters

Shortly after taking off and uncertain of what I had just heard, a chill ran up my spine. I don't recall which airport it was, but prior to COVID, I was traveling routinely nearly every month to some state or another to talk about PD. The tune, "I Did It My Way," sung by old "blue eyes" started to invade my thoughts between prayer supplications of God, please don't let us die.

As we began our ascent, having just left the runway not long before, I heard a loud boom followed by a deceleration and drop in altitude, then came a sound as if something had detached from the plane. A noise like that is never a good sign. I have seen too many movies, and *Die Hard* quickly came to mind. As I tried to muster the courage to look out the window to see if the engine was still there, I glanced briefly at the flight attendants who were now standing near the cockpit. They, too, had startled looks but tried to conceal them when they caught me looking their way. Realizing I was squeezing the arm of the young man sitting beside me, I apologized and gently unclenched my hand. There was no need to ask if he also had heard the sound. The look on his face was one of terror.

This only made me more apprehensive since he was a man in uniform. Certainly, he had witnessed a thing or two. This did not bode well. I had hoped it was one of those auditory hallucinations but to my chagrin, it was not. For the first time, I was not pleased with the notion. An auditory hallucination would have been a welcome relief. It seemed I was not that fortunate. Could this be my end? This served me right: the family had begged me not to go on another trip since I had just recovered from another medical scare, but as usual, I took it under advisement and went anyway.

Interrupting my thoughts, the captain's voice came over the speakers. I was expecting to hear something like we are turning around, brace for emergency landing, etc., but rather in a matter-of-fact voice he told the flight attendants to take their seats and for everyone else to stay seated. I thought the situation was much more serious than that. Apparently, he did not want to panic anyone since we were all going to die.

The plane began to shake. I took a deep breath and began to count, waiting for an impact. I dared not look up. With my head bent down, my prayers intensified as did my motion sickness, yet I saw no need to reach for nausea medicine. I would most certainly die before the medicine took effect. I soon realized nothing else was really happening, despite the plane continuing to shake vigorously. Neither did we seem to be losing altitude. It felt like an eternity had passed before I gained the courage to look out the window. With only one eye open, I peered out and expelled a huge sigh of relief. The plane's engine was still there and appeared to be working fine.

I have been traveling for thirty years and have experienced flights with mechanical failures, trouble with landing gear, nails in the tires, trouble taking off, and sitting on the runway for five hours during a blizzard on Christmas Eve. That particular event ended in having a Secret Santa exchange party on the plane with everyone opening their gifts and food items and passing the champagne around. But never had I experienced anything like this before. This was entirely different. Even my very first flight going off to college was not as anxiety provoking as this flight. To this day, I still cannot recall where this happened.

Having flown through many pockets of turbulence over the years, I know the routine. But this undulating pattern which shook the entire plane felt different. The most bizarre thing is that neither the captain nor crew made any mention of it being an abnormal occurrence. Nothing like, "This is your captain speaking. Sorry, we are experiencing some turbulence. We are going through a patch of rough weather, sorry for the inconvenience." *NOTHING.* Not a single word during the entire flight or even after we landed. The crew had also acted weird. After a while, everyone seemed to relax. I finally reached for my medicines since my head was about to explode. Despite the initial adrenaline rush, I was happy that the plane was able to withstand whatever was going on.

Everyone on that plane must have been holding their breath because I don't remember hearing a single sound, or perhaps it was the galloping of my heart that muffled any other sounds. It seemed that for a time the cabin was completely silent. I believe everyone, like me, was waiting to see what happened next. Once everyone felt secure, the chatter throughout the cabin increased. Just then I chuckled at the thought that perhaps no one told me this was part of a movie, and I was an extra in a dramatic plane scene.

By this point, due to stress, my dopamine was flowing like a river of lava, and I could feel myself becoming hyper and giggly. As happens frequently, medical emergencies occur during intense stress and unprecedented events. Good to know some things never change. Sure enough, there was a medical emergency on board. A flight attendant called for a medical person to come forward, and I wondered if I would have to deliver a baby, as I usually ended up doing during disasters—even though I hated gynecology in med school. I seemed to be a magnet for helping pregnant women in their birthing. The last delivery I had performed was during a hurricane in Houston, standing in water up to my knees. As I hesitated to stand, thinking whether it was a good idea to volunteer, fortunately, someone else also volunteered and assisted with the emergency.

Finally, we arrived at our destination, and I felt as if all the passengers around me had become family. I was home, although late, I could breathe a sigh of relief. I was back on familiar territory and in one piece. I thanked God for having landed the plane safely. No sooner had I finished praying when I saw security guards and police officers sprinting in the same direction I was heading. What now? I muttered. Then someone said, "You must turn around; we have closed this area." Everyone started walking briskly around me as more officers headed in the direction I was going. Really? I just want to go home. I turned around as we were instructed, and I began to pick up the pace to try and find an exit away from the commotion. Here we go again. God protect us! All I wanted to do was be in my bed next to my husband. I tried calling my mother and my husband but got no answer. I couldn't even talk to anyone to say goodbye. "Figures," I muttered under my breath.

Eureka! An exit! After I finally exited the airport and found my way to my brother's home, I was able to stop shaking and catch my breath. I never had been so happy to be alive, even if I had to live with Parkinson's for the rest of my life. One must also remember that in life, despite having friends, family and loved ones, you may at times find yourself all alone, as I did in this scenario. The only thing that will keep you going is your inner faith and convictions in a higher power. Because no matter who you are, no one can take away your beliefs. Living with Parkinson's is sometimes like going on a flight like that, thinking you are going to die, that you have reached the end, but miraculously life changes and you find joy and laughter again and want to keep fighting and living until the next scary moment.

But you must remember to keep moving, going forward no matter how dark it is around you. Even if it feels like it's barely one step at a time until you find your way again.

CHAPTER 6

Que Será Será . . .

"For I know the plans I have for you," declares the Lord, "plans to prosper you and not harm you, plans to give you hope and a future."
— *Jeremiah 29:11*

The song made famous by Doris Day was one of my dad's favorite songs to sing to me. Whenever I asked him about my future, he would say, "*Que será será*, but it will be a good one, you will see." My dad was always so proud of my achievements and thought I was a great doctor, as only the eyes of a father could see.

I had only been in this country for seven years and despite going back and forth between Houston and my hometown back in Mexico, due to immigration laws, I never finished the first, fourth, or fifth years of school. Not knowing more than a handful of words in English, I was placed in regular classes in junior high. Of course, kids can be cruel and frequently harassed and made fun of me for not speaking the language properly. Once I got the hang of the language, I still had trouble with spelling during spelling bees in front of the class each week when I felt completely humiliated and extremely incompetent. I had huge trouble with *ch* versus *sh* sound for instance. When I began to have symptoms of Parkinson's it affected my language making it slower, less fluent and decreasing my vocabulary in English prior to taking medication. I acted very much like an aphasic patient who can speak without hesitation or impediment in their native tongue but lose ability to speak in their second language. I only thought of this because when I am off levodopa or on a minimal dose, over the years I have reverted to having a thick Hispanic accent for many words. I had noticed but did not pay much attention or think it was a big deal until my daughter was visiting and I said some words and she began laughing. She then added that I am the reason she mispronounces so many words. There was no good come back from that other than I really have to up my levodopa doses, so my language is not ruined for others that are listening to me speak.

Although I never got a failing grade, I was not accustomed to being less than a stellar student. My father played a huge role in making sure I succeeded. He would troll garage sales and buy me old grammar books and elementary reading books and found a vintage box of 500 basic vocabulary words to begin building the foundation for the English language. I was always good at math, which was my saving grace. By the end of eighth grade, with God's grace and my father's help, I was inducted into the Junior Honor Society. My super smart best friend Kim, with whom I remain close friends to this day, talked me into applying to a Vanguard program for high school. Since I had only been speaking English for three years, I did not think I would be able to do well on a cognitive test and get into an extremely competitive school in Houston. But somehow, we both got in and continued to push each other, both of us being ultra-competitive and goal oriented. We both aimed to go to one of the top northeast schools. She is now a physician, which she claims was because of me. She got accepted to Columbia but went to Georgetown in DC which is not far from the City of Brotherly Love.

I owe Anna Maria. Not only for getting me into the University of Pennsylvania (Penn) but also introducing me to the major that would pave the way to my future career, endeavors, and passion. These in turn were the foundation builders for the advocacy work that I have been involved in for the last twenty years. She was also instrumental in recruiting my two dearest friends Pati and Nellie, who became my roommates during senior year and who have remained my close friends until this day.

The exciting new field of study being offered at Penn was known as —BBB (biological basis of behavior) with three different concentrations. The first one focused more on the social aspect of the brain and integrated with sociology and other social sciences; the second one was more psychologically oriented; and the third one was a combination of the anatomical function of the brain with behavioral presentation—mind versus the brain, in a nutshell. At this point in life, I was really interested in social studies and sociology. All my aptitude tests consistently pegged me as a sociologist. I love sociology so much that I wish I had gotten a minor in this field. I had enough hours as an undergraduate. Despite this interest in social studies and sociology, my focus centered around the neuroscience arena, which was rapidly becoming a growing passion.

Nevertheless, my aptitude for the field of sociology caught the attention of one of my professors who loved my work so much that she submitted it for publication. To this day, I continue to work closely together with the School of Social Work at Stephen F. Austin State University. It was here along with my friend and dean of the department, Wilma Cordova, where I began my work on using faith as another tool in the armamentarium to bring physical and spiritual healing. For years I was a frequent lecturer at the *Faith and Trauma* conference held at the university annually to help others live a full life beyond their ailments using spirituality.

It was my friend Pati, who introduced me to her high school friend Ricardo, a medical student at Hahnemann University, where I ended as a medical student. I learned that when God wants you to do something, He will get you there, He will put all the pieces and people together, even an old boyfriend to get you where you need to be. Remember that when He calls you or wants you to be involved in something, the naysayers do not matter. Only what He and you think matter.

CHAPTER 7

Let's Battle

*"A bend in the road is not the end of the road. . . .
Unless you fail to make the turn."*
— Helen Keller

The spirit of perseverance refers to the quality of being determined in the face of challenges. Many in my family will tell you that there is no one more capable of standing defiant in the face of adversity or a challenge than me. I'm not sure if you know the movie *Michael*, starring John Travolta who played Michael the Archangel. As you may recall Michael is the spiritual warrior who led the battle to throw out Lucifer and the rebellious angels from heaven, and is the one who will also lead the fight against the dragon (Satan) in the final days in the end of time. He is continuously waging war against evil and is often depicted with a sword in his hand. However, in the comedic fantastic movie, Michael is an angel who is portrayed as being less than angelic and living with an older woman in a motel. He has many vices and one of them is his love of sugar, right up my alley. I used to steal sugar cubes anywhere I found them, usually at the entrance of grocery stores, where coffee was readily available for customers to help themselves. I would grab a handful and fill my pockets with them. Throughout the day and sometimes several days, I would pull out one by one full of crumbs and fuzz from my coat pockets to suck on. Like his character in the movie, I, too, love sugar. According to my husband, I also love to do battle. Okay so I like to argue. Maybe I should have been a lawyer instead of a physician?

It is unfortunately a family trait. Plus being Hispanic does not help.

When family gathers everyone talks in a forceful manner. Now, I have two voice volumes. Soft when at home, the reason why it is so hard to speak on the phone much these days. The other is my loud voice that happens when I get happy or excited. This is the reason why I can still do public speaking without many difficulties because my passion triggers dopamine to be released sometimes so much so that I get louder and louder with excitement. At least I don't need a microphone to be heard. Unfortunately, having PD and other illnesses can make voice modulation difficult to control, especially when irritated or excited. Sometimes my strong personality compounded with lack of frontal lobe filter can give an appearance of me wanting to engage with horns fully ready for battle.

Once, in a zoom meeting, someone took my words out of context and became angry, I tried to change the topic and diffuse the situation, but this person would not let it go and went so far as insulting me. Needless to say, the embarrassment and the frustration caused my voice to get louder and louder. My daughter who was in the next room came over and gave me a sticky note saying, "Mom, you are yelling!" When I read this, I got my bearings back knowing I could not control the volume of my voice, I just simply stopped talking. Now I try hard to first be well medicated which will decrease tongue slips and decrease irritability and when I feel my voice escalating sometimes out of sheer mania and excitement, I pause take a deep breath and recall my daughter's note to stay in control of situation.

There was one time I was struggling with excruciating migraines, which usually is not the case because medications work but for whatever reason I could not get the medication from the pharmacy, and they were giving me the runaround. Three days into the headache, I was about to lose my mind. Why I did not go to the emergency room, I am not sure. In any case, I was very sick, and I needed to go back to the pharmacy and wanted my husband to go for me, but he had other fun plans, so I had to go. I was so upset that I glared at him in such a way that he knew he better than to stand in front of the car, or I might consider running him over. I was deeply ashamed of this thought and grateful he did not stand in my way. I got to the pharmacy, how, I am not sure, but the first words I heard were, "We do not have . . ." and I burst into tears from pain and frustration. This is the one and only time I have ever lost control in this fashion, and I was deeply embarrassed, but my breakdown somehow miraculously produced the medicine at no cost. If I had known this was the strategy, I would have employed this tactic sooner. The point is that sometimes you must defend yourself and get upset to keep from being run over.

After getting into Penn and changing my mind to attend medical school, I encountered many obstacles from the advisors themselves during the process of writing letters and getting ready for medical school interviews. All I kept hearing was, "Don't apply because you won't get in," basically because I was a Hispanic woman. Fortunately, I didn't listen and got into several medical schools and even got accepted into two dual programs as a PhD and medical student candidate. I had applied to a PhD program on the insistence of my mentor. However, at that time in my life, I did not see the value in prolonging my career further since I planned on being a clinician. This is one of the few regrets I have and where God was directing me, but I failed to carry through. I feel I might have still been able to do more research had I had the proper credentials.

Then, during the second semester of my first year of medical school, I was diagnosed with my first serious medical condition, an autoimmune disease, which now thankfully is in remission. At the time, I thought my life was over. I was hospitalized and missed a big chunk of the second semester, including a whole set of exams. When I returned, there was a small section left to cover and a final exam for each class. Given my precarious condition, the board offered me leave to return in the fall as a first year again. I was not about to start over. They gave me a weekend to think about it and decide. I spent the weekend resting, reflecting, and praying and went full steam ahead, determined to take my chances. Thankfully, by the grace of God, I was able to pass all my exams and proceed to second year on schedule despite my weakened immune system.

As a specialist, I had to fight the stereotypes against women physicians, especially as a Hispanic woman. I had many confrontations with colleagues who felt they could walk all over me, but I was able to mark my territory and be trusted and respected in my community. It has been an uphill battle, but every step of the way, God has had the upper hand and saw me through.

Even when I chose to become a movement disorder specialist, I knew where I wanted to go, but the position I was considering was filled at the time. So, I took another job until my husband finished his training and then I could reapply.

Parkinson's was to be my destiny. Halfway through the year, I called the program director and discovered there was an unexpected vacancy, and the coveted spot was now mine. And so began my journey with Parkinson's.

Remember you can always be victorious, but you must first be ready to do battle. It is of equal importance to know when to engage in war and when to abstain. This is what I have learned from my lived experience with Parkinson's and life. According to the *Art of War* by Sun Tzu "if you know the enemy and you know yourself, you need not fear the result of a hundred battles." Having had to live with multiple illnesses my entire life has taught me to sift all the garbage from my life and cultivate spiritual traits like love, joy, peace, kindness, goodness, faithfulness, patience, and self-control. I have come face to face with the person in the mirror and I am at complete peace as to who I am flaws, defects and all. What makes me stand strong in the face of changing winds and adversity is my complete and total confidence that the spiritual sword and shield forged by God through all these years of suffering is of impenetrable strength. So, like Michael, whether the fictitious archangel or the real one said to have defeated Satan in the heavenly war, I will be ready for battle until my dying breath.

CHAPTER 8

How Do You Solve a Problem Like Maria?

"Unpredictable as weather, . . . she is gentle, she is wild. . . ."

—— *The Sound of Music* by
Oscar Hammerstein and Richard Rodgers

When I think of *The Sound of Music* I think of my grandfather immediately, for it was the first movie he took me to see, just the two of us. Of course, who can forget the well-intentioned but handful novice. Not long ago, I went to my first Parkinson's retreat in South Dakota. It was held in an old abbey. Outside the convent was a huge lake and rolling green hills and all I wanted to do was run like Julie Andrews singing "The hills are alive. . ." I believe that my friends from the retreat recognized the fact that I am a bit of a conundrum. I don't seem to fit into any given box and as my husband has said many a time, "The only thing predictable about her is her unpredictability."

It seems I have always been an enigma, a paradox if you will. For starters, it seems that wherever I go, even if I am from that place, I am always confused as being a visitor in the country or state. I have been thought to be Persian, Jewish, Italian, Spanish, French but never Mexican or American. Go figure. The only people that embraced me as one of their own were the French during my visit to Paris, which thrilled me because it meant I had learned French well enough to converse with the natives. Perhaps it was the small trace of French blood I inherited from my maternal great-grandmother.

Yet, my name always seemed to precede me somehow. Apparently, somewhere in the world is a famous Maria De León. A prominent female neuroscientist expert in dementia and Alzheimer's. I frequently receive letters inviting me to talk about this field because of her work. However, not long ago, I kept receiving invitations to head a consortium of experts in dementia at a prominent conference in Europe, assuming it was for the other Dr. De León, I ignored them. As they kept insisting, I finally replied and told them my field of expertise was women and Parkinson's, and to my surprise, their response was, "We know. We want the Parkinson's Diva!" I was certainly flattered and humbled at the same time.

One of my closest friends told me not long ago, "I have never met a doctor quite like you." I am as much a right as I am a left-brain person, I equally love fashion and the arts as I do neuroscience. I am bold and daring. However, I was never so outspoken as I am these days. I think that is due to Parkinson's which has made me more truthful with less filter. Especially when I'm off the dopamine. Yet it's interesting how I am *more* daring when I am fully loaded on dopamine than I used to be as a younger person. I know exactly where my daughter gets her adventurous side from. I believe the last time I tried something so bold was a few years before my diagnosis — I went hot air ballooning; although the whole time I kept trying to measure the distance and calculate the odds of survival should the balloon malfunction and we crashed.

As a child, I was afraid of everything. These days not much fazes me, but you probably will not see me jumping out of a plane anytime soon like I wanted to do before PD. I have learned to deflect, change the rhythm and the dance steps, but I have never stopped the music from playing. Yes, I would not be human if from time-to-time certain diagnoses had not caused me to pause for a second and ponder my existence. Yet, most people around me probably never even noticed a hint of what was behind the smile. Perhaps they noticed I withdrew a bit from the public eye or from a project but never for too long.

A few years ago, doctors thought I had a third type of cancer which was thought to be much more aggressive than the previous two I have survived. Thus, it was potentially more deadly. This time I initially felt a bit scared and worried I might not live long enough to see my daughter graduate, in part, due to my husband's consternation. He has been through so much with me since the day we got married. I, of course, am used to my health issues being like a roller coaster, up in the morning and down in the evening and topsy-turvy all day long. I typically don't even bother calling the doctor, I just rest and wait for the storm to pass. I know my body so well, especially as a doctor, and when I sense something is potentially serious, I make my way to one of my many specialists' offices. At times it is quite a challenge for me to figure out the source of the problem with so many medications and medical issues, but as a clinician, I can typically narrow down a diagnosis. Although it is getting harder and harder to know which doctor to call first or what the problem may be given the extent of my medical history and plethora of medications I consume. On occasion, there are emergencies that require a hospital admission or an ER visit. Nevertheless, they are the exception rather than the norm. Thank God for this.

But these past two years have been unusual. I visited the emergency room five times in four months. One of those visits resulted in a surgical procedure, preventing me from flying to Portugal which saddened me deeply, since I had my heart set on going. Fortunately, my illnesses did not keep me from delivering my talk to movement disorder specialists around the globe with the likes of Dr. Ray Chaudri and Dr. Blas Bloem. Even after the last hospitalization, medical intervention, and receiving IV fluids for severe dehydration, I still managed to attend a Parkinson's talk held in San Antonio in April of last year. I was particularly swimmy headed from fatigue, lack of nutrition, and intractable GI bleeding. But through the grace of God and the support of my husband and my mother who took me to speak despite their protesting, I managed to deliver a semi-cohesive talk both in Spanish and in English. On top of this, I found some strength to do tai chi with my friend Julie. Footage of me practicing tai chi, speaking, and getting ready in the convention center powder room is now immortalized on film in the documentary *The Only Day We Have* by Vanessa Reiser, as were the beautiful bruises on my arms. I am surprised I did not topple over before I made it back to the hotel that afternoon. There is something to be said about the power of God and running on adrenaline.

But I got ahead of myself a bit. I have discovered in life that the things you worry about are never the things that derail you and stop you in your tracks. As I said, everything was going as usual, I was about to have a big milestone birthday, and we had plans to travel to San Francisco. Then I get the news of a possible third malignancy. *Here we go again,* I thought. If my husband hadn't shown such overwhelming concern, I probably wouldn't have become so worried. He is the calmest person you have ever met. He rarely lets anything frazzle him. Only twice before had he gotten a bit of a jolt that caused him to drive above the speed limit: once when I went into premature labor, and the second when I was told I had recurrent cancer and was summoned to Houston the same day.

I felt as if I had just told him about the news over the phone when he was already at the front door. I had had so many ailments a few months prior to the news, and I was still unable to hold much food down due to the nausea and vomiting which then triggered the pain. Although, few people ever mention this, there is an increased risk of developing a rare type of cancer of the gall bladder with Parkinson's disease. It is more common in women of course and only 30% live more than a year after diagnosis. Unfortunately, I am aware of a young Parkinson's patient who died due to this type of cancer.

My husband is a radiologist and panicked immediately at the findings on my imaging scans regarding this possible third malignancy. And when he becomes overly concerned, it is serious business. I know the prognosis is grim, maybe facing the final curtain when he begins to show signs of public affection. As a physician's wife, I can get second opinions faster than most, but this time I could not get a consensus of what this could be or what to do next, and with every study and doctor's visit, the prognosis grew worse. Stress levels for both of us kept increasing with each passing day. We had connections to the number one cancer center in the world — MD Anderson. I have worked there in the past and know how dedicated and committed they are there, but the experts in this type of cancer were out on vacation for the summer and the first possible appointment for me was two months down the road. With this type of cancer, every minute counts.

The wait was going to eat my husband and me alive. But we prayed and put our faith in God and decided to go on a planned family trip to San

Francisco and celebrate my birthday. We were all together and enjoyed different aspects of the trip. My husband, being a history buff, really enjoyed the visit to Alcatraz. I enjoyed sitting in the courtyard feeling the breeze and admiring the view. The entire family enjoyed the visit to Muir Woods and walking among the magnificent 100-year-old red oak trees. I believe we all felt such immense awe and simply basked in the serenity of the forest while we enjoyed the pure unaltered beauty and fresh air. Just what the doctor ordered.

But I suppose I should have paid more attention to Mark Twain's remarks, then quoted by Hemingway saying, "The coldest winter he ever spent was a summer in San Francisco." Although no one is certain who said this initially or if it even was San Francisco. However, having been there several times at different times of the year, this observation was dead on. Nevertheless, it did not detract from the beauty despite the heavy fog. My birthday, which did not start on a good foot with nausea and vomiting in bed, did end on a positive note culminating at one of Frisco's five-star French restaurants. Had it been up to me, I would have eaten there every day.

During that time, I was offered a chance to fly to Boston and be in a photo shoot for a Parkinson's awareness campaign, against my husband's recommendations, but I decided to go rather than wait at home for the curtain to drop. As I often like to say, might as well since I was not doing anything. So rather than sit and wait at home, I took off to Boston. That trip turned out even better because, by pure coincidence, I was able to reconnect with an old friend I love dearly but had lost track of for many years. I was in a lot of pain, and I could not really enjoy the wonderful food the team provided, which was a total shame since I am a huge foodie. Yet, I did not let this impact me one bit. I still managed to have a blast, especially seeing behind the scenes of a filming production, and meeting new filmmakers and producers.

I love movies. I took several film classes as an undergraduate at Penn, and it was there that I had a chance to dine with several actors and producers over the years like Sylvester Stallone (even was an extra in one of his films), Edward James Olmo, Jack Klugman, and Aaron Spelling to name a few. I think I have always secretly wanted to be a movie star and a model. Even with my crazy life, God has always been true to his word "Delight in the Lord and He will give you the desires of your heart" (Psalm 37:4). This protracted season in my life allowed me time to reflect on all the things I was grateful for. Now every time I see a production, I have a newfound appreciation and understanding for the inner workings behind the scenes. My husband, who is a big jokester, started getting me Core water bottles because I mentioned this is what they had on the film set, and he calls it my "modeling water." I get a big kick out of it, too.

Not knowing what my future had in store, I was embracing every moment. I began to take stock of my life and despite all the lows, I had much to be thankful for. I chuckle a bit when I ponder the fact that my guardian angels have been working overtime trying to take care of me. They would probably sigh in huge relief if they no longer had me to look after. My husband thinks I am like Benjamin Button, getting younger with age. I am not sure about this, but I know it is a dang miracle I am still alive all these years after almost being kidnapped, killed in a crossfire at a mall, killed in a drive-by shooting on a freeway, interrogated by the FBI, and stalked by a psychopath which put the fear of God in me for a long time. Yet, I can be grateful for my life and know for sure I have lived to the fullest, always seizing every waking moment as if it were my last.

Not long ago, I asked my brother what three words he would use to describe me.

"Three words are not enough," he'd muttered, then added, "I need an entire dictionary!" After careful consideration, he said, "Insatiable would be one."

"Really? Really?" I uttered back, half in disbelief. I never thought he would think this. "Why does everyone say this to me all the time? Am I that difficult and painful to deal with?"

He chuckled a bit. But did not give me an answer. After having heard this word used to describe me many times over the years, I had to do some serious introspection. The first time someone said this to me, I was deeply offended and felt like the person was saying I was too needy or clingy. But, after hearing this term over and over through the years, I was curious to know the reason why so many people thought this about me. I mean, I know

I am a handful (according to my husband, "More like a PITA — pain in the a**," and he laughs) especially now that I live with so many illnesses. Geez, I am really a Diva?! Wow! This was news to me. As I have gotten older and sicker, I guess I have turned up the dial of my divaliciousness in some unconscious way because my outings and interactions with people are further and further apart with long periods of isolation. In medical school, I had a few close friends, but somehow, most of my classmates knew what perfume I wore. It was a hoot one day in brain anatomy class when a picture of Elizabeth Taylor's Passion perfume in its iconic purple bottle was shown to illustrate the olfactory nerve, nearly one half of the class sitting in the lecture hall in unison said, "Maria," and many of them turned to look at me. It was crazy. I could not believe people recognized my scent. Funny, I don't recall telling anyone what I wore. My husband jokes that the only time I have been upstaged by anyone was a person suffering from a manic disorder (although mental illness is not a laughing matter). Interestingly after seventeen years of living with PD, I now have a tendency to get manic on levodopa, especially if I am doing something I truly enjoy. It is an unusual high and is hard to control. I feel as if I am about to burst at the seams. Especially since I don't go out much these days when I do, I become overjoyed, which makes me extremely loquacious. This over-the-top personality, fueled by Parkinson's and combined with an extremely curious personality, is why I am defined as insatiable. I guess all those years meeting with my grandfather's clients of all walks of life made me more outspoken once I got past my shyness. As my daughter noted, I have three voices: a Mom voice, a Maria voice, and a Dr. De León voice, which is the most assertive.

I consider myself a bit of a visionary who is never satisfied with the status quo and thus always looking to improve things around me, starting with myself. Nevertheless, this constant search for knowledge and truth and improvement does not mean at all that I am an unhappy, discontented person. I am very secure in who I am and who my God is, and I draw strength from that knowledge. I try to use my flaws as well as my virtues to bring happiness and hope to others. Because I attempt to live life as fully as possible, I also want those around me to share in the experience, especially my loved ones, which as my brother has said, can be tiring at times. Fortunately, or unfortunately, I am becoming less tiresome since I am slowly running out of steam. My body is beginning to feel the effects of years of disease and because I must juggle so many medicines, sometimes my *umph* is no longer there even to visit with my dearest of friends. However, I am lucky they come to me so often when I am not able to go out or drive.

But just like I survived that potentially devastating cancer with God's grace, I will continue to thrive as long as He allows. I have been sick most of my life. When I was born, my parents were told I would never walk, I guess even as a toddler I was determined to overcome challenges. That unbridled strength of will is exactly how I live my life. I approach every obstacle as an opportunity to learn, to grow, and to change the world and myself.

This is why it's so hard to keep up with me at times because my mind is constantly analyzing things, particularly in medicine. As my brother said, I always want to do things, experience things, and live to the fullest. I am a bit like George Bailey from, *It's a Wonderful Life*, full of optimism and dreams with ideas of how life should have panned out. But life had other plans. I thought I knew what I would do next year and the year after that and so on after I became a movement disorder specialist. Even after I closed my practice, I thought it would be a matter of time before I reopened. Yet despite all my best efforts, this has not come to fruition. My once ardent dream of being a physician has been put to rest and new dreams have sprouted out, redirecting my path, allowing me to fulfill my initial desire of why I became a neurologist – helping people with Parkinson's and bringing them hope. Had it not been for my own personal journey with PD, more than half of the things I have done would not have been feasible, starting with the emergence of the Parkinson's Diva.

Always remember to believe in yourself, and even though there are plenty of things in life that will scare the living daylights out of us—from silly things like spiders and thunderstorms to huge things like illnesses—the best thing to get through them is to follow Maria's advice and think of all the things that makes us happy, like "Raindrops on roses . . ." I think about the times spent with my grandfather when I am feeling sad, and then I don't feel so sad. What do you think about to avoid feeling sad?

CHAPTER 9

Angels in our Midst

"Do not forget to show hospitality to strangers, for by so doing some people have shown hospitality to angels without knowing it."

— Hebrews 13:2

We all know that having Parkinson's can cause some brain fog where one is awake but not fully cognizant of all the decision-making steps required for a successful transaction. I suppose this was my state of mind when the incident that led to the next day's mysterious events transpired.

After days of going back and forth with my family about details regarding my nephew's graduation, my family, as is their customary style, notified me of their plans at the last minute. At the eleventh hour of the night before graduation, I found myself frantically trying to find lodging for our weekend stay. No sooner had I finally completed my itinerary than I got a call from my sister saying plans had changed. I was already irritated with the whole ordeal and wanted to simply scratch off my attendance. However, I was going to help my nephew move and caravan with him back to my home afterward. I was high on stress, to say the least, which never bodes well. I have a very tight margin of equilibrium in which I function, and it does not take much to alter it. Thus, rendering me less reliable and accurate in my decision-making capabilities. This inability to multitask amid stress and chaos has been the reason for my persistent absence from medical practice. I literally turn into a brunette with no brain. My daughter knows that I must be in complete relaxation and fully on dopamine before any serious conversations can take place. Before any important discussion takes place at home, both she and my husband are mindful to inquire about my mental status and decision-making abilities.

My daughter learned this from a young age when I would give her inaccurate information or plain silly answers to school-related questions such as, "Who are the three Musketeers?"

"Michelangelo, Donatello, and Leonardo," I answered her matter-of-factly as I was driving her to school late, still in my pajamas, and seeing double. Sometimes I feel I could lose my head if it were not attached or be so confused . . . like the time she woke me from a deep sleep because it was time to go to school.

I was startled from my bed at the light suddenly shining on my face, staring glassy eyed at the girl by the light switch at the bedroom door, wondering who the heck she was.

She said, "Come on, we are going to be late."

Still trying to get my bearings, I asked, "Where are we going?"

"School," she replied.

"I don't have school," I replied and turned over in bed. But just as I did, my brain fog and confusion lifted at the same time I heard . . .

"Mother."

Obviously on days like these, the right brain did not know what the left brain was doing. During this event, I think I found myself in one of those instances of experiencing an alternate, surreal universe. Thank God for divine intervention. I am still not sure what happened that evening or the following night, which is even more puzzling because I am usually able to recall all my silly comments, actions, and behaviors during my off times.

So here I was, completely exhausted mentally and physically, dealing with family . . . and the thought of an arduous weekend ahead drained me even further. As I said, it was nearly midnight, and I called to cancel my prior hotel reservation as I searched for a new hotel. I made reservations at a Hilton hotel near Commerce, Texas. Keep in mind I am a rewards member and have years of traveling experience. As always, I wrote the address and phone number and reservation number. Because it was so late, I did not receive an email confirmation, but I was not too alarmed since I had all the correct information written down. I even wrote down the name of the clerk I had spoken to just for good measure. And I headed to bed to try to sleep because it was going to be a long drive and an even longer two-day weekend carpooling and packing my nephew's apartment after graduation.

After only a few hours of sleep and having taken all my medications, I set off on a five-hour drive in a car full of people. After some minor inconveniences, we got there just in time for graduation. I had hoped to be able to rest beforehand and check in at the hotel early or at least lay down for a while since I have chronic back pain. None of this was possible and, as always, the chairs in the stadium were so uncomfortable. After a lovely lengthy ceremony, I was already running out of steam. I needed to refuel and take medications to go on. After dinner, we went back to his apartment to finish cleaning and loading cars which took much longer than anticipated, and it was now nighttime. I was already dragging plus it was black as onyx outside, and no one else but me could take the wheel. My nephew had his little truck loaded and was following me. We finally arrived at our hotel destination, and everyone jumped out of my van ready for a good night's rest. However, it would be a few hours before we would be resting. In all my crazy life happenings, this night remains as one of the most bizarre and unexplainable to me.

As soon as we arrived in the hotel lobby everyone plopped on the sofas while I proceeded to the front desk to check in. Little did I know that I was about to be hit by a storm seen only in the desert. It was nearly midnight; I was nearing empty on dopamine. On top of it all, I was extremely migrainous and experiencing severe back pain—on the border of losing control if I did not lie down to rest soon and take all my medications. Trying to muster enough energy, I shuffled up to the front desk to check in and tried to smile and keep my desperation in check. The agony would only increase in the next hour.

I gave my name and my reservation number to the clerk. She said there was no such number.

"Oh?" I said, trying to contain my frustration. I asked if this was the Hilton Hotel Green at the address I had. She said yes. I asked if the phone number to this hotel was correct. Yes. I asked if they had a clerk by the name I had listed on my paper, and she replied affirmatively.

"Good, he is the one I spoke to last night." Thinking we were finally making headway.

"Well, no," she answered, "he was not on duty last night."

I felt as if someone had hit me with a brick. I could hear in the background my family beginning to murmur and get upset, especially my mom. I asked the clerk to look at my name again and offered a different spelling, oftentimes they misspell my name or take out the space in my last name.

"Perhaps you made reservations at Hilton Green in North Carolina." she said.

"Uh? What? Why would I have this address and phone number?" She called that hotel, nothing.

I finally asked if she had any available rooms to which she replied, no, because of graduation and being a holiday. I felt helpless and confounded wondering how this came about and feeling guilty putting my loved ones through this ordeal. As I watched, my family sprawled out on the floor looking at me for answers as my eyes filled with tears. Since everyone was dependent on me, I had to be strong, although I called my husband and broke down for a few seconds, which proved futile, since he did not provide me with any real support or answers to my questions and current predicament.

I had no energy to drive home, which was at least five hours away or anywhere for that matter. I was beyond exhaustion. To make matters worse, it was Memorial Day weekend, and the chances of finding a vacant hotel nearby were slim. Plus, I had no willpower or stamina left to go on a hunt with two vehicles stuffed to the rim, three young people half asleep, and an elderly woman about to lose it as well. I was at my wits' end. I was a second away from having a meltdown when my phone rang. I never answer my phone if I don't recognize the caller, especially if it says unknown. Yet this time, I answered . . . perhaps because I was so distracted.

"Maria?"

I became suddenly very still and wanted to say, *Is that you God?*

The friendly man's voice on the other end asked, "Are you still there?"

"Yes. Who is this?" I asked.

"I was so worried about you not coming in yet that I decided to call you before I went home. Are you still planning on coming tonight?" I was totally perplexed trying to understand what was happening.

"Who is this?" I asked again. He gave me his name. I inquired once more. I was still trying to piece things together in my brain fog.

"I am calling from the Comfort Inn where you have reservations."

"Comfort Inn!" I exclaimed. There was light at the end of the tunnel. *I might finally get to sleep in a bed tonight,* I thought to myself. I was too tired to put the pieces together, so I asked, "Where are you located?"

He gave me an address which did not pop up on my GPS, so I started to worry. He gave me other landmarks along with the restaurant where we had dinner earlier that evening, but I did not recall seeing a hotel there. It was not far from where we were, and we did not have much to lose by going to check it out. Nevertheless, I asked the front desk clerk who really felt bad for us if there was such a hotel across the freeway. She said she thought there had been a new one recently opened but was not certain. I got directions from the gentleman on the phone and off we went. Sure enough, there was the Comfort Inn. Looking very quiet since it was past midnight, we went inside, hoping no one would steal anything from our cars. Inside it was quiet and dim but an older gentleman stood there and greeted us with a big warm smile.

"I am so glad you made it in. I was so worried," he said once more. "I have both of your rooms ready, all you need to do is sign. You must be exhausted."

"You don't know the half of it," I replied. "Do you work here every day?"

"No," he answered. He was not the man I had spoken to on the phone when I made reservations. "But something told me I should come in tonight and call you to make sure you got in safe. Now that you are here, I can go home."

We said good night, and I thanked him. Still puzzled, I had gotten a surge of dopamine dealing with the enigma of how this mess had occurred. We went upstairs for no more than five or ten minutes and when we came down to the lobby to get water, the elderly gentleman was gone. The next day, I inquired with the front desk attendant about the nice gentleman that had assisted us in the wee hours of the night because I wanted to thank him and leave a note of commendation since he had rescued me (us) from despair. She looked a bit bewildered, then said there was no one working at the front desk or at the inn with that name. Then she added that there used to be an older gentleman at the inn when she started working, but he had retired several years ago. She did not recall his name. How could this gentleman call us and get us checked in? Plus, a woman was supposed to be working the desk that night.

To this day, I have no other explanation but to believe it was an angel that helped us.

So, as we go through life, let us remember never to fear for there are angels by our side.

Hard to Be a Woman

Sometimes It's hard to be a woman with PD.
You'll have good times and many awful times as well, but
   you will keep smiling
'cause, after all,
It's hard to be a woman
Living with PD.
But sometimes that's all you've got –
Doing things that make no sense to anyone but you
Because it is hard to be a woman with a disease that makes
   no sense
So you will continue to stand tall
And show the world who you really are!
Parkinson's, you are no match for me!

A Song

(to rhythm of "Bohemian Rhapsody")

Is this the end? Irritability, stiffness, slowness, shakiness
   too?
Sweaty nights, dry crackling skin, mascara running down
   my cheeks . . .
Someone please grab me a fan.
Seems I am losing all my friends.
Parkinson's is battering me.
I don't know if I should laugh or cry.
Ooh, ooh, ooh . . .
am I to be just another poor girl with PD?
Mama, good night, but I won't sleep.
Now my pants are all stretchy . . . Someone please tell me
   where the potty is!
Am I cut out for all this drama?
Please someone tell me where the chocolate is!
Ooh, ooh, ooh . . .
I am just a girl who likes her heels.
I keep smiling.
Yet, my neurons are all dying, and my purse is full of pills.
Is this what my new life is to be?
It really does not matter.
What will people say or think?
Nothing really matters.
If I am not here tomorrow. Carry on, carry on . . .
For all that really matters
is what's inside of me.
Nothing really matters . . .
But me.

CHAPTER 10

That's Life

"You can't always choose the path that you walk in life, but you can always choose the manner in which you walk it."

— John O' Leary

"That's Life"
by Kelly L. Gordon and Dean Kay relates:

I've been a puppet, a pauper, a pirate, a poet, a pawn and a
  king /
I've been up and down and over and out and I know one
  thing /
Each time I find myself flat on my face /
I pick myself up and get back in the race. . .

Twice when summoned back to Mexico to get our permanent visas we discovered the consulate had run out of permits. Out of the first six years of schooling, I only officially completed two from beginning to end. This constant set the groundwork for my resilience in living with multiple progressive and neurodegenerative illnesses.

My first time experiencing this feeling of losing energy and momentum — like walking through molasses — was during a trip to the casinos in Las Vegas. My legs kept getting heavier, my feet harder to lift or even place in front of the other. It became harder to keep my head upright and my shoulders back. Despite all my effort, I was completely frozen in place. I couldn't take another step. I desperately needed someone to put a big key inside me and wind me back to normal. But after resting a while on the floor, I was able to pick myself up, start moving again ever so slowly, and make it back to the hotel. At times, I have been confined to bed for months, unable to drive for a year, unable to think clearly, dress myself, or even walk on my own without any assistance. But each time this happened, I was able to get back up again, not by my own strength or will, rather by the strength I receive from my faith and the power of prayer. Especially the constant prayers from my mother and my church family. Each time I fall, or new challenge comes my way, I simply utter "That's life!" My brother described me best when he wrote this poem (shared with his permission):

> *Skip the beaten path and blaze your own trail, this is not a reference to my sister's driving but how she truly lives her life. Although her vehicles say otherwise. Bebzie, as I like to call her, does not wait to be inspired by others but finds her inspiration from life itself. Bebzie is always planning 3-4 activities ahead of everyone else. She has an endless desire to do and experience everything she possibly can. Parkinson's has not diminished this one bit. Sometimes this can be exhausting for those of us along for the ride, but every minute is filled with joy and laughter. It is usually very late at night when she succumbs to her weary body. This is the time I truly enjoy her company most of all. This is the time we can share and reflect in so many ways on how we are so alike. It is these times that I wish could last forever. And yes, this is when she is lying down exhausted and tired from the day's adventures — nearly always involving watching movies, indulging in good food, and making a late run for something chocolatey. With sleepy eyes, she'll turn and ask, "So, what are we doing tomorrow?"*

CHAPTER 11

The Physician

"And though you study medicine for a score of lifetimes, there will come to you people whose illnesses are mysteries..."
— The Physician by Noah Gordon

ong ago, during my first few hours as an intern covering the ICU, I recall looking frantically around the room for a doctor to assist a family visiting their loved one. This is because the notion of me playing the role of doctor had not fully taken root. I had just spent the last twelve years fighting everyone to get to this point, and now I was unsure.

The very first book I read the summer before starting medical school was *The Physician* by Noah Gordon. Recently, I watched the movie where Ben Kingsley plays the role of Ibn Sina, the professor and mentor of the story. It is still inspiring with pearls of wisdom for those who want to practice the art of medicine. I have always said that medicine is both an art and a science and what distinguishes a great physician from a mediocre one is not the knowledge but the care and interest he or she bestows upon patients.

As the family drilled me for answers, anxiety and trepidation took over, making me wonder if I had what it took to be a good physician. Yet, I was determined to do my job to the best of my ability.

Over the years, I have grown into my role and become much more at ease in dealing with life and death matters, dealing with the needs of the families, and giving support to the caregivers. I owe my growth as a physician in part to my mentor, friend and colleague, Dr. Mya Schiess, and my experience as caregiver to my grandparents and father. My grandfather suffered from vascular dementia, my grandma battled Parkinson's disease, and my dad developed a rare skin cancer Merkel's carcinoma. The time I spent giving 24 hours a day care to my invalid grandmother was an eye opener for the love, patience, skills, and commitment required to care for a person with a progressive disease. It's exhausting, even when there is financial, physical, and emotional support. After a year, my nerves were frazzled, and my marriage had essentially been put on hold. I had no time or energy left to dedicate to my spouse after caring for patients all day and coming home to care for two children — my daughter and my grandmother. I cannot even imagine what it would be like without support and resources. Yet, despite the exhaustion, I would not trade a single moment I was able to spend with my grandmother.

The circumstances not only brought me and my daughter closer to her, but the experience significantly enhanced my professional life. The time spent caring for her produced in me a deeper compassion and empathy for those suffering as well as sharpening my listening skills, learning to read between the lines when patients and their caregivers spoke, allowing me to become a much better physician than I was previously. As my career unfolded, I gradually realized that even with all the knowledge and medical advancements, there were times when my efforts to provide healing and comfort seemed insignificant, like a fleeting gust of wind. It was during these moments that I truly understood that the true power lies solely in God.

I believe every doctor should be a patient at some point during their training. This firsthand experience would truly help them grasp the frustration, humility, loss of dignity, and loss of control when one is submitted to a battery of tests, uncertain results, receiving an unwanted diagnosis, and then being asked to wait for the next steps. By having our blood drawn repeatedly or asked to take pills multiple times a day, we could learn what it's like to be poked and prodded and treated like just another member of the herd. We should experience what it's like to be left completely defenseless and as vulnerable as a child. Only then can we begin to understand what it is like to be a patient and what is required of a physician to give comfort and to learn from the example Jesus provided us when treating the infirm.

We often forget and take for granted that when we treat a patient, we hold the soul and not just the body in the palm of our hands. In Noah Gordon's novel, *The Physician*, the protagonist, Rob Cole, reflects on the profound impact of medical intervention with the thought:

"To feel somebody slip away, yet by your actions to bring her back! Not even a king had such power."

I was given a special gift. I could somehow detect who would succumb to their illness and who would survive. Try as I might, I could not reverse the course. I never could understand if it was because the patient gave up, their disease had advanced, or if it was simply God's will. Maybe it was just their time. I will never know for sure. Nevertheless, I discovered that the best treatment was to make their last days as full and positive as humanly possible, so they could die with dignity and peace.

When it came to predicting the progression of someone's illness, my father was the last person I could confidently assess. I knew his time had come. It was so hard to accept, and we did everything we could, but in the end, as always, it was God's will. I spent every second by his side to make sure he knew he was loved. He had a very peaceful death. One which was bittersweet to see him go, but I did not want him suffering anymore. He had lost all quality of life. So not only did I lose my father, but also one of the few people who truly believed in me and my gift as a doctor. I would take him to his dialysis or to his chemo and he would look at another patient who was suffering with a neurological illness and would turn to me and say, "Oh, how I pray you get better soon because they need you." Tears would trickle down my cheek, and I would hug him and know he was the best dad ever. I am glad that I got to spend every minute with him throughout the last year of his life.

So even though I can't practice my God-given vocation in the traditional setting, He has allowed me to continue with my calling to help people with chronic intractable illnesses live full lives beyond their diseases. I think both my grandparents and my dad would have been proud if even one life was made better because of my work.

However, becoming a doctor was not a walk in the park due to the constant naysayers who thought that because I was a woman, I could never achieve such lofty dreams. On the other hand, I also met many

Hispanic women along the way who regretted giving up on their dream and encouraged me to not give up on mine. I am truly grateful for these women.

God kept me in medical school despite my first serious illness and helped me defy the odds. Upon receiving the fellowship I had desired by way of a twist of fate, I thought I was set. Then the real test of being a doctor came.

First, it was learning to stand on my own two feet in the face of death while holding on to God's hand. The challenges came from other physicians who acted like I was dispersing black magic. I was cast as a sorcerer of sorts by asking for patients to be referred to me or the ER immediately upon signs of stroke, so treatment and rehab could begin immediately. I was even given a book on neurology because someone thought I did not know what I was talking about. I was almost lynched when I introduced the use of Botox for my dystonia patients. Had it been the time of the Inquisition, I am certain I would have been burned at the stake as a heretic!

Then came the constant fighting tooth and nail for patients who were deemed neurologically impaired due to delirium or *status epilepticus* but truly had surgical abdomens and were at risk of dying if surgery was not undertaken. Fortunately, because of my unwillingness to let someone suffer, two patients were brought back from the brink of death.

Then there were the nutty patients, the dysfunctional families, and finally, the roller-coaster insurance world. I never knew you needed to be a psychoanalyst, a marriage counselor, a social worker, or carry a law degree to navigate the world of medicine. Plus, the martial arts skills needed to defend against the seemingly frail elderly people who can barely move and talk but can pounce on you in a second if they perceive you have said the wrong thing.

Thank God my first office had two entrances into each exam room. That design literally saved my life. During a regular consultation of a Parkinson's patient, my sentiments changed drastically from one of sadness to fear within a blink of an eye. He sprang across the room with the force of, scooping me off my chair in one deliberate move pinning me against the door.

After this, my staff and I kept tranquilizer darts on hand and a Queen Square Hammer, as a defense tool during my training at the TDC (Texas

Department of Corrections). Despite many early setbacks, my practice quickly grew. I felt competent in managing Parkinson's disease and advising families as to expectations of the illness. However, after spending only a few weeks caring for this vivacious woman with end-stage Parkinson's, I knew I was in over my head. Here I thought I was the expert in dealing with PD, yet the magnitude of the task was enough to overwhelm even a so-called maven. I wondered how my patients and their families ever managed to live with this disease on a daily basis with little complaint. I quickly came to understand that living with a chronic illness was not for the faint of heart. Furthermore, the things that wear on a care partner day in and day out are not the things that doctors necessarily focus on.

It's the daily struggles a caregiver goes through in grooming a loved one who is completely rigid, restricted to a bed, or the roller coaster of emotions that occur as their loved one exhibits cyclical mood fluctuations from happy to sad to angry and distrustful, all within a matter of minutes. This lack of steadiness and consistency in one's life slowly chips away at the layers of our soul. Eventually, if not careful to replenish our spirits with things that nourish our inner being through prayer, meditation, and social connections, we are doomed to become devoid of emotion. For this reason, I began encouraging patients and caregivers to do something for themselves that brought them joy, like spending time with family, friends, or anything that could bring balance and well-being.

Even before my grandmother became bedridden, I needed someone to stay with her during the day while I worked. As her illness progressed, I also needed help on the weekends, which meant a constant parade of therapists and nursing aids at my house. Never did I imagine that I would have to supervise fights between my toddler and grandmother over a toy or that I would have to raise two children simultaneously, albeit at opposing stages in life. I discovered that it was much easier to handle my daughter simply because of her smaller size. I could not simply pick Grandma up, as I would my daughter, to carry with me to the office or on rounds.

But as all children do, they both enjoyed stories at bedtime as well as coloring, playing card games, and listening to music while singing along. These activities served to calm my grandmother when she became agitated, but also the interactions between a great-granddaughter and her nana helped establish a lasting bond. After applying these same techniques to the care of my patients, it also resulted in fewer altercations in their homes.

What I never could have imagined was that my grandma's illness would turn me into a domestic kitchen diva. Before caring for Grandma, cooking was always an afterthought. And since she was an excellent chef, especially in the pastry department, her hallucinations usually consisted of baking and cooking. I began cooking to appease my grandmother. She would get upset if I did not serve what she spent *all day cooking*. It was exciting when I got her recipes just right and she would acknowledge that her cooking that day was superb.

It was fascinating to observe the inner workings of her mind. Having always been a great cook, even in her mental state, *abuela* continued to do what she always loved to do for her family — cook. She measured and whipped and decorated all those wonderful pastries she had made a thousand times in her life. Except now it was all in her brain. Loving her as much as I did and because she really was cognizant of most things happening around her, I could not bring myself to tell her there were no cakes or anything to eat after dinner. So, I would try to replicate her concoctions and made home-cooked meals more often. During this period of my life, I began to fully appreciate the huge emotional impact a disease has on a family. The financial factors which play into the decision making of whether a person should be cared for at home or placed in a facility usually come at a great price, leaving many people feeling guilty. Caring for Grandma caused a change in the dynamics in my home, straining my personal relationships. I slowly began recognizing the same sheer exhaustion and helpless look in the eyes of my patients' caregivers and other family members as I started to hear the frustration in what was being unsaid.

I realized, thanks to my grandmother, that I carried the responsibility of not only healing the infirm but also providing counsel and comfort to the loved ones to a greater extent than I had been trained to do. I allotted time for patients and caregivers alike by finding an outlet together and separately so they could continue focusing on their relationship rather than seeing their new role as an unwanted intrusion in their lives. I encouraged everyone to focus on building positive memories while providing them with tools to improve their situation, reminding them that whatever was happening in their lives was sure to pass. Asking them to focus on the good when confronting a difficult situation, even if it was just a once-weekly outing for an ice cream cone. I also learned the hard way to never tell patients they could no longer drive and left that up to the Department of Public Safety.

Recently, a colleague asked me if I thought the stressors in my life, especially at the time of my symptom manifestation, had played a role in its development. I had often pondered this question myself since many people in the healthcare field appear to develop PD. Although there are no accurate statistics, there seems to be a higher incidence of physicians and other health workers such as nurses and dentists, to develop the disease. We know that stress lowers your immune system and causes greater inflammation. Given my other immunological diseases, and how much people in the medical field suffer from stress this certainly could make sense. Food for thought.

Let's learn to practice relaxation and meditation. Say *yes* to the things that nourish your spirit, body, and soul, and *no* to those that drain it. Make time for yourself.

CHAPTER 12

The Patient

"Man, when you lose your laugh you lose your footing."
— *One Flew Over the Cuckoo's Nest*
by Ken Kesey

I have discovered that the reason patients are seemingly so unhappy with their doctors is because often, they are treated as a collection of symptoms and diseases rather than persons with souls, dreams, and desires. We are complex beings with insecurities, flaws, in need of love and understanding, especially when confronted with our own mortality. Far too often as we cross the line from a healthy individual to one living with a chronic condition our sight becomes constricted, losing the ability to look at the whole panoramic view. We then proceed through life with blinders, only focusing on what's directly in front of us such as our losses, our pain, and our struggles. However, we need to be reminded of what it is like to be alive.

The reason any of us seek medical attention in the first place is in hopes of stalling or reversing disease so that we may continue to live life to the fullest. Life moves on despite living with a disability, or a malady. Thus, we must embrace love, friendship, dreams, and family for these are the things that anchor us and give us courage to face adversity. The best way I have found to foster our own happiness and well-being is by developing a heart full of gratitude. It's too easy to forget to give thanks for being healthy until we are no longer in good health. But it is even harder to be content and grateful when your body and soul are aching.

At the end of each day, I like to make a mental note of at least one thing I am grateful for (you can also keep a journal or put the blessings in a jar to review at the end of each year). It does not have to be a big thing. Sometimes our blessing may be just simply making it through another day. When we focus on the positive, we become empowered and able to face setbacks a lot easier. Even when the career you had fervently worked on comes to a screeching halt, as mine did after receiving the all too familiar diagnosis I had dispensed to so many patients before. The way I was able to continue on and reinvent myself was by reminding myself that everything happens for a reason. God is always working behind the scenes, even if we don't see it right away.

Someone once told me that it must be so easy to work at a doctor's office. Anyone can do it. All you have to do is sit there, answer a few calls, collect a copay, have lunch, and go home by five. If only it was that easy, then anyone could be a healthcare worker. There are crises to be handled, insurances to be dealt with, fires to put out, charts to be reviewed, labs to be checked on, drugs to be called in and that's just the peak of the mountain. The smoother an office runs, the harder everyone is working behind the scenes. Same for parents and God.

I saw a cartoon once of a mama mouse holding the hand of her little one walking hand in hand. The mother's tail was covered in mouse traps and the caption said, "See, Mom — there was no danger." We don't recognize the one watching over us until something bad happens to us or we are wiped out by an unexpected storm. This is when I like to remind myself that storms are not always a bad thing. Sometimes, they serve to clear the path for something better to grow or flourish. This Parkinson's storm certainly has done this for me over the last two decades. An example of unexpected and unwanted storms are the yearly-occurring fires. Although on the surface they cause so much damage they play an important part in the evolution and continuation of our forests. In Yellowstone Park, there is a different type of pinecone than the ones we have here in East Texas. They are called lodgepole pinecones (*Pinus contorta*). These cones, unlike other ones we are familiar with, remain attached to the trees for nearly twenty years, and even when they fall, they remain completely closed. They only open when they meet extreme heat then they disperse their tiny seeds that possess papery wings that helps them disperse. Thus, when a forest fire is ravaging the other pine trees and their cones, the lodgepole cones remain closed, holding the key to new life and reforestation after the fire has passed.

After a few years of constantly trying to position myself as a trustworthy physician in the community, my practice grew very quickly thanks to God's grace who brough Mark into my life. I believe he single handedly built my reputation. God put him and his wife Janet who is now one of my dearest and closest friends in my path as I was finishing my fellowship at Baylor and moving to East Texas. He was born and raised in the town I was moving to and was thrilled to not have to drive to Houston any more to see a specialist. We hit it off from the start. He told everyone he met to come see me as a doctor and he was a well-known, well-respected member of the community. I became a national and local speaker for several pharmaceutical companies, yet I fostered a deep desire to help the Parkinson's community on a more personal level.

I thought I would be practicing neurology for the rest of my life, especially since all my paths had led me to this profession. But referring to *Ecclesiastes 11:5*, we know that God's ways are as mysterious as the wind. Since my practice was flourishing so rapidly, I had invested in a new office which was specifically designed with Parkinson's patients in mind. Little did I know it would serve me as well, as I began to develop symptoms. Funny how life is, Parkinson's was the reason I became a doctor and a neurologist. Parkinson's was always a favorite topic of conversation so of course when I was diagnosed it took my family years to realize I had now become one of those patients I always spoke about. Since my childhood I had been learning to walk with God and with every new situation and tribulation my faith had grown. However, when everything is going well, it is easy to become complacent and for prayer to become more of a routine, but all this was about to change as I faced another chronic illness—this time a neurodegenerative one. I was about to find out how strong my faith really was. Had God led me to become a neurologist through all those struggles and hardships just to leave me hanging halfway through? Had all my sacrifices been for not, I pondered? However, I have learned that not a single leaf moves without

God's knowledge or consent so everything that happens to us and around us has a purpose.

While trying to wrestle with my own diagnosis and wondering what was in store for me God was already busy at work behind the scenes. He had bigger plans for me that extended well beyond the walls of the hospital and my office. However, as I embarked on a new journey with Parkinson's disease, this time as a patient, I realized I would need all the skills I had learned as a doctor during training. I had to wait on God to show me the next step. Funny how the things that you worry about are never the ones that end up throwing you curve balls. Rather the things you least predict to happen usually change your world and turn things upside down. Who would have thought that my passion and love for the brain and neurological diseases would be my *raison d□tre*? Soon, the challenges I had faced as a medical student and as a physician would pale in comparison to the obstacles I would have to face as a newly diagnosed Parkinson's patient and that was just the beginning. Being a patient made me realize that I am even more impatient when in need of care than I ever was. I always say be careful what you ask for because you might just get it. I have always seen impatience as one of my biggest flaws. Thus, I used to arduously pray for gobs of patience. Well guess what, I got a disease that makes my mind and body move like a sloth where being impatient only makes things worse. Plus, I got a few other diseases that have been tempering my character and disposition ever since. The first thing He did was make me bed bound for several months. There is nothing worse for an impatient person that is used to going a hundred miles an hour to suddenly have to stop and wait for others to help. Boy was this hard but learning to be still to listen to God's voice is the first step in obedience and being a person that God can use.

I know some people do not like to be referred to as patients. I can understand especially when in need of attention and care amid suffering, one can be less than willing to wait for tests results, diagnosis, and medication or treatment to work to make us feel better. My own journey as a patient began with learning to be patient. Interestingly, the usage of the word *patient* when referring to an infirm person dates back to 1382. Geoffrey Chaucer first utilized it in the story of the doctor in *The Canterbury Tales* to refer to someone receiving medical care. I deeply believe there is no other word in our vocabulary that fully describes the state of an individual who is forced to live with a lifelong disease. Trust me, after living with PD for nearly two decades along with a whole slew of other chronic illnesses, I have resigned myself to the idea that there are days I have no other choice than to live one day and sometimes one breath at a time. Focusing on the here and now has taught me the true meaning of the word "patient" in its original context to suffer or bear, derived from the Latin word *patiens* from *patior*. Not losing sight of the forest for the trees while learning to maintain some dreams and goals alive I rely on God's grace to get me through one day at a time.

My first lesson in patience came as I tried to figure out what was going on with me. No one has less time to be sick than someone who is a full-time physician running a solo practice, building a new office, and raising a toddler. There were too many people depending on me, yet I had to go through nearly every test short of a brain biopsy and spend three years of my life seeing doctor after doctor, trying to put a name to my condition. The roller coaster of emotions brought on by anticipation and constant letdown was at times worse than the disease that was beginning to take root in my body. The ordeal made me realize that even the most trivial or inoffensive doctor's request can result in undue stress and cause major anxiety and burden not only to the person undergoing the testing but also to the entire family. I recall ordering many MRI scans over the years. There were many people who were claustrophobic; thus, I tried to be as accommodating as possible while still obtaining necessary tests. However, it was not until my own personal journey that I soon came to detest such tests for myself as well. The mere thought of enduring another MRI makes me cringe, especially as I have become stiffer, slower, and a bit larger in girth. Aside from taking necessary medications before any procedure or test, I have learned to control my heart rate through a sequence of exercises which involve inhaling deeply and exhaling slowly until my breathing and my heart rhythm are the same. The best thing about this mindfulness or breathing relaxation is that it can be done anywhere.

After my diagnosis of PD was confirmed, I thought, no problem, I got this. I have treated lots of patients with this illness and took care of Grandma for years. However, I quickly learned that making a diagnosis and treating the disease is much easier than living with it in your own body. For starters, I learned that even the slightest side effect can wreak havoc on an individual more so if attempting to hold a job and raise a family. Never mind the effects medications and disease can have on the body of a young woman. There were many times, I felt that the medication side effects were worse than the disease. Even after three years to finally get diagnosed, it took me another year and a half to find the proper treatment regimen to allow me to continue to function as a mom, a wife and doctor. I have done well controlling my disease considering the many years I have lived with it. Yet, even when I reached 100% normalcy, this state never lasted very long. As years have gone by this feeling of complete normalcy is getting shorter and shorter each time. Although when fully on, I am nearly 90% of what my prior capacity used to be. The problem is that I only achieve this about 50% of the time. This reduction in time is hard to deal with because I have a tendency to want to do everything when I am normal. Thus, I end up overcommitting or overexerting myself. Although I am learning to say no to a lot of things and limit my commitments, it is still difficult to do especially when I feel strong and able.

The first five years after my diagnosis with PD were a complete blur since it seemed that the heavens opened the window and sent a downpour of infirmities all while trying to keep my marriage, my practice, and raise a neurodivergent child. I am truly blessed that somehow by God's mercy and grace I was able to keep it together and raise a fine young lady. Because I had such little energy and was under constant brain fog, I stopped taking calls and slowly began to decrease my hours at work. Since I like to find the silver lining in things, having Parkinson's forced me to spend a lot more time at home which meant seeing my daughter grow up.

As a working mom I was often conflicted about leaving my child alone. Especially when you have a smart daughter who knows how to pull at your heart strings by saying things such as, "Why do you have to go see patients?" "Because they need me." "I need you, too." I am proud to say that despite all the ups and downs I only missed two events in her life. I loved being a mother, every bit of it although a manual would have been helpful at times especially when you have such a smart inquisitive child.

However, before I could be comfortable in my own skin, flaws and all, and find the real me, I had to learn humility, obedience, patience, and perseverance. I experienced an interesting stay at the hospital. My short stint to get treatment for a recurring thyroid cancer reminded me of a scene from *One Flew Over the Cuckoo's Nest*. Because of the radiation treatment required, I was placed in an isolation room with a small window overlooking the roof of the hospital. My door had a small window covered with a shade that looked like it had not been washed in years. Because I was restricted to where I could walk, I could not look out into the nurses' station or hallway. Within the door, there was a small slot at the bottom akin to something one would use to deliver mail. *Would they be sending me cards?* I chuckled inwardly at the thought. However, I did not quite grasp why this slot was there initially.

Since I was radioactive. I could not have any objects that were not disposable. Thus, I did not have any electronic devices for entertainment, plus I was restricted to walking to a small area within the room which was covered in newspapers and plastic. The TV remote and bed controls were also covered, which made them even less functionable. Each morning, I would get the five-minute call from the nurse to see if I was still alive and inquire if I had taken my meds. My stupor, feeling like I was on fire, and deep boredom was interrupted daily for about thirty minutes when the alien as I called the nuclear medicine physician dressed in a hazmat suit, came in to administer my radiation and check on my radiation levels with his Geiger counter. He never uttered a word. His task involved handing me the radioactive pills which came in one of those containers you might see in a sci-fi movie, frozen cold and oozing with smoke. Otherwise, I was completely secluded. This went on for a week.

I could have died, and no one would have known until the following day. I felt like I had been transported to one of those psychiatric wards I deeply detested as a resident. No wonder many times when I made rounds on those wards, I would get startled as I tried to peek into the patient's room only to find them staring back at me peering through those porthole windows. I probably would have stood there, too, staring out of that tiny window in my room trying to catch a glimpse of life. However, I could not even walk past half of my room to get even near the door to look out the window. I lay in bed wondering if the nurse from *One Flew Over the Cuckoo's Nest* was the one in charge of this ward. I would hate to get an accidental frontal lobotomy to boot. Apparently, the head nurse here did not possess any type of pleasant demeanor or disposition because during my entire stay she never once asked, "How are you? How do you feel? Can I do anything for you?" The phone would ring at exactly 7:00 a.m. and before I could utter a word out of my burning mouth from the effects of the radiation, I would hear the voice on the other end.

"Did you take your pills?"

"Yes!" And before I could say another word, she would hang up, never to be heard from again until the following morning.

As I said, the miniscule room had one door, the one with the mail-slot opening at the bottom. I was admiring it, wondering why it was so low and what it was used for, when suddenly someone shoved a food tray through it and pushed it hard toward me with a long stick. I began to laugh at what I had just witnessed. Laughing and shaking my head, I couldn't help but ponder about prisoners in solitary confinement. It made me realize that I was in a similar position. But unlike a prisoner I had not even been read my rights. They could at least step outside into the courtyard. I guess I was in solitary confinement for bad behavior. The first meal tray remained out of my designated area. So, I had kneeled and stretched my arms to reach the tray. Remember, I have Parkinson's disease and had only been diagnosed less than a year before and I was in no way, shape, or form controlled plus I had severe thyroid problems which meant, this was no easy feat. I am not sure how long I lay on the floor, trying to grab the tray, and then trying to pull myself up from the floor. If only I had something to write with, I would have sent a note back to the nurses' station asking when my sentence was going to be commuted.

As if this humiliation and seclusion were not enough, the bed broke, as did the TV remote control, basically the entire apparatus so even if I wanted to call for help or adjust the bed, I was completely out of luck. Unfortunately, I could not get a replacement or have a tech come fix the problem due to my contaminated state. After enduring that fiasco, I should have liked to at least get a superpower. After all, isn't that how villains and superheroes get their powers in all the comic books? I am still waiting for my superpowers to develop. Flying or teleporting would be nice.

At any rate, I am sure that the staff could have borrowed a hazmat suit to fix my bed if they had been thoughtful and caring. Fortunately, since I was so lethargic and stuporous, I endured my confinement and was let out for good behavior after a grueling seven days.

One night, as I lay in the dark half asleep, my entire room began to light up. I was turning into a human torch. I was literally glowing a nice teal color. So much light filled the room that I still don't know if I had an out-of-body experience or simply hallucinated from so much radiation. I felt myself floating out of my body toward the ceiling and suddenly it opened up toward the sky. I recall seeing the night sky and the stars twinkling and feeling a cool breeze. Then a sudden burst of light occurred which blinded me, and the sky became blue for an instant, and it was daytime again at which time I felt I was having a conversation with God asking if I was going to die. I don't recall hearing anything nor an answer given. However, I was unexpectedly overcome by a deep sense of peace and a feeling of being at home. The bright light diminished gradually, and I began to feel myself floating back into my body into the bed. I then opened my eyes to look out the window through the blinds which were partially open, and I could see it was still nighttime. There was a sliver of light piercing the darkness which was coming from the roof top of a nearby building. The next morning when I awoke, I recalled my experience, wondering if it had been a dream or something else. I felt certain that somehow, I was floating higher and higher into the sky until I felt I had reached heaven and tears of joy rolled down my cheeks. Even now when I think about the experience it remains so real and still gives me a sense of peace and well-being. I still believe I had a conversation with God, although I did not hear His voice. I had the feeling someone had eased my soul and told me all would be well and not worry about not being there for my daughter.

I have never been quite certain if this event was a hallucination caused by the tumor effect, by the Parkinson's, and/or the radiation. Perhaps it was a true encounter with the divine. But no matter what the cause was, my convictions and faith grew more that day. Immediately after, I felt an incomparable peace fill my soul. Although I still had to face surgery, I knew I would be okay. Sure enough, by the time my husband and I went to the surgeon about removing the recurrent tumor near my carotid, it was no longer found, and I have been in remission since then.

Lately, I have been going through a lot of medication changes due to a severe allergic reaction to many of the compounds I have been on for years. I suddenly started breaking out in with a huge, itchy rash all over my body. Some of the sites were extremely painful. This latter part was of concern since there is a rare allergic reaction called Stevens-Johnson syndrome and could be deadly. Once again, I was dismissed by some of my doctors including my dermatologist, who is a professional expert whose job and responsibility includes diagnosing and treating this potentially life-threatening illness. Talk about a double whammy. This was a combination of pure aggravation and frustration combined with an incessant itch that was turning my skin brown and scaly with streaks of purple, particularly on the abdomen. In the upper right and left quadrants of my abdomen I was experiencing purple streaks that got worse with time since they began to be a source of severe pain. My prognosis looked bleak according to my differential. I began eliminating medicines one by one to get at the root cause. Fortunately, I got my endocrinologist's help who started me on medications to help the pain and ease the rash. It took over six months for the rash to get under control.

As one would expect, by altering a well-oiled machine, taking things out, and putting in new things, it caused my entire system to truncate. Even before the rash disappeared completely, I began to have lupus flare-ups, and my Parkinson's symptoms went haywire. On top of the already complicated scenario, the new medications used to replace the ones we had stopped caused even worse side effects with gait, which involved excruciating pain relieved only by narcotics.

Shortly thereafter, I had a follow-up visit with another of my many specialists. I could barely take two steps without feeling my legs buckle and give out on first attempt to walk. When my name was called, I struggled to stand up. Finally, with great effort, I somehow hobbled into the exam room.

The nurse upon seeing me exclaimed, "My goodness, you look like you are in a lot of pain. I have never seen you look like this before."

I uttered, "I believe this new pain is a side effect of the new medication. I am afraid it fixed the problem that I had before but replaced it with a worse one."

"I am sure the doctor will fix you with a new treatment to get you feeling better soon." I smiled and offered a thank you as she walked out of the exam room. Within minutes, the doctor came into the room and told me that I looked fantastic, in fact better than ever.

Giving him a smile, I uttered, "I am worse than I was before. I am not able to walk. I think the new medication is the culprit."

Of course, he gave me a side glance, quickly adding that he was, "100 % certain that it is NOT the medication. Perhaps it is that other thing they say you have. Do they still think you have Parkinson's?"

"Unfortunately, it is not going away," I replied, not wanting to argue about whether or not I have PD or any other nonsense. Yet, I so wanted to resolve the issue of severe pain I now had since the addition of the new medication. "The pain is so unbearable I had to resort to pain pills. I can't live like this," I said.

Because I was insistent on trying something different, I was given a new medication which works well without impairing my mobility. The pain went away magically when I stopped the medication. This scenario confirms the importance of keeping diaries, and letting others know when there is a problem.

Remember that good communication between you and your medical staff, family and caregivers is key. Be your own advocate. Pay attention to your body and write down any changes, especially when new medication is introduced. "Be joyful in hope, patient in affliction, faithful in prayer." (Romans 12:12) Keep either a written diary or a video one. This serves two purposes. One, it allows you to focus on what is going well and not so well. This allows you to think about the causes—is it something internal or external? Two, it will help your medical staff focus their attention on those issues to improve your quality of life.

CHAPTER 13

Troublemaker

"They say before you start a war you better know what you're fighting for. . . And I wanna live, not just survive. . ."

~ *"Angel with a Shotgun"*
by Alex Marshall, Alexander DeLeon,
and Evan Taubenfeld

You could say I am a woman who leads a life of danger, but not by choice. Trouble seems to find me wherever I go. With the number of death-defying situations I have found myself in throughout my life, I think my guardian angels are yielding their swords just to protect me. I am sure they will be glad when God relieves them of their duty. Since I was a child apparently, I got lost a lot because I tended to wander away and sneak out of my grandparents' house through the small space between the bars in the window. A neighbor often summoned my mom that I was at their house or brought back to my grandma's house. According to mom, I got lost in Guadalajara as a toddler and was missing for hours. God only knows where I went but I was found in a park sitting by a tree. I still like to sit near trees and be mesmerized by their leaves.

As I got older, I tried not to wander but that is just my nature. But it seems that with age came more dangerous encounters, some initiated by my curiosity, but the majority occurred just by chance. I did all my schooling up north, but I got homesick and returned to Texas for all my training. During a short span of time cars have literally flown over me while driving down the Houston freeways like some surreal movie scene waiting in slow motion to see the outcome. Three times to be exact and then another time when I had just moved to my town in East Texas. Then there were two incidents in which I had a rifle pointed at me, one on the freeway and the other one occurring at my favorite mall. Inadvertently, as my family exited the mall near closing time, we stepped into the middle of a shoot-out between an officer and an escaped convict. Of course, I was the one directly in in the line of fire. I had herniated my disc, and I was in severe pain. I also had severe weakness in my leg, which was the reason we were there in Houston. I was holding my child's hand; she was only a couple of years old. I was dragging, so when I stepped out, I had my head down. Hearing something *pop*, I immediately looked up.

I am not sure what I expected to see but certainly not a police officer with a drawn gun shooting straight in the direction I was in with my daughter. My husband was more to the side and oblivious. I yelled at him to duck and take cover. I grabbed my daughter shielding her with my body. I don't know where I got the strength to carry her until we got to the car, and we hauled as* out of there as if we were robbers.

There is no doubt miracles happen, and guardian angels exist. I saw the officer shoot his gun right at me or my direction just as I looked up. In all these instances, I have managed to come out completely unscathed by the grace of God. Now I get to share my life stories with you.

Those who know me best say I live in my own rose-colored world. Perhaps it is not that I don't know bad things are happening around, but I choose to believe in the kindness and generosity of people. Being a summer baby I love to spread sunshine. However, that is not to say that all my life experiences have made no impact on me. Although I still believe in love, kindness, forgiveness and second chances, I am much more analytical when evaluating behavior and motives of people.

Since I appear to be a magnet for trouble my friends and family have forbidden me to travel alone abroad lest I cause an international incident and end up like Bridget Jones in some foreign jail and no way to get extradited, since I have no connections to high-ranking officers or diplomats.

How and when all my mishaps began, I'm not sure. But somewhere around the time I was in medical school I think I inadvertently positioned myself on a Persons of Interest list. To be honest this is when my Parkinson's disease began to take hold in my brain; so perhaps my judgment began lacking unbeknownst to me putting me at risk by not properly recognizing potentially dangerous scenarios. One ordinary day, the FBI suddenly showed up on my doorstep, asking about some criminal case involving a stolen vehicle. My first thought was that this was a prank by one of my friends who was always trying to set me up on blind dates. So, when I saw this very attractive young man claiming to be a federal agent, I did not believe him. I was still very young and naïve, and I had never seen a special agent badge. So how could I know it was not fake? It turned out to be a real badge, a real agent, trying to solve a real crime. Sadly, my life was so boring spending all my time at the hospital, I was quickly eliminated as a suspect. What was unnerving was that I had been followed for a while, and I was not even aware of it. I am sure that during that initial investigation, all my life history was placed in the system and has remained there ever since.

A few months later, after this initial visit by an agent, it seems the scary incidents began to occur—and still periodically happen, much to my chagrin. On an ordinary Thursday afternoon when I was still a medical student, I wanted to go to the movies, but all my friends had other plans, so I ended up going to an earlier show by myself in downtown Philly. Funny, it was a good espionage movie starring Harrison Ford. Shortly after I left the theater, it exploded from a bomb — reason unknown. I was grateful my friends had opted not to go, or we would all have been there at the time of the incident, and I might not be sitting here recounting stories.

Things started happening more frequently once I moved back to Texas. When I moved to East Texas during a mandatory routine background check for hospital staff privileges, I got a call from the hospital saying that I had a warrant for my arrest. I had to go through a whole ordeal to clear my name. My life would have been so much easier had I been a traditional wife and taken my husband's last name. He never lets me live this down each time I get into trouble due to my last name which apparently is an extremely popular surname in Texas (and here I thought I was special). But for many reasons, I am deeply attached to my name. Maybe if I leave the state of Texas again things will settle back down, who knows? Maybe worth the try. And I will become anonymous once more. Although my husband and daughter think I am way past that stage since I tend to run into people I know wherever I go.

Parkinson's has had a huge role in me become notorious, in my opinion. However, if you ask any of my friends or family members, I was unique and special since the day I was born. One of my good friends told me not too long ago that since she met me, she knew I was different and special. She had never met a neurologist like me.

Ever since I developed Parkinson's, I set off airport alarms all the time. I am very tired of being patted down and stripped searched, so much so I have considered getting a DBS or pacemaker just so I can carry a card that says I don't have to go through those X-ray scanners. It always is the left side where my Parkinson's disease began and continues to be the more affected side that triggers the dang alarms. In all my years of having the disease it has been a handful of times where I was not forced through a mandatory pat down. Interestingly the ankle where my foot dystonia began remains the culprit area that sets off the alarms and scanners the most. Maybe I should say I have pins in my leg. But then if they X-ray me, they will find none. What is a girl to do? Get a wheelchair? Perhaps.

The last pat-down took place in Barcelona.

"Ma'am you have to raise your arms higher and spread your legs wider."

"I have PD. I cannot go higher or wider."

What follows then is a little bit more harry when security thinks you are carrying something suspicious in your bag like some contraband rather than a ball of cheese you just bought there at the airport. Thank goodness I could only carry one ball of cheese—because they were heavy. I would have looked even more suspicious if I had bought all the ones I wanted.

"We are going to have to look through your carry-on bag."

"Great. First pat down, now bag search," I mumble under my breath, sweating like a crazy woman again. I glance at my family, observing the puzzled expressions on their faces.

"What do you have in your bag? There is a big round thing." (I'd forgotten about the cheeseball I had just purchased.)

"Oh, I have a peach."

"No, it is not a peach," the security officer responded, yanking my carry-on bag from me. She opened the bag and pulled out the big solid ball of Manchego cheese wrapped in black paper.

"Oh, that." I smiled when she pulled it out of the bag. "That's cheese."

She looked at me and asked, "How does it taste?"

"I honestly don't know," I replied. "I just bought it."

Not being satisfied with my explanation, she inserted a needle to do an analysis. Looking at her, I am not sure I want to eat this cheese anymore. In the meantime, my niece is carrying a boat load of butter in Tupperware containers, and no one said a word. Thank goodness I did not get any ham.

But before this incident we had to go through the boarding phase on our way to Spain for the Parkinson's World Congress. We were waiting to board the plane. My husband and I were on one side of the aisle, while my daughter and niece were on the opposite wall waiting to board. As we neared the podium, I saw a couple of in-flight security officers coming out of the jetway which we would be using. They were two or three young men wearing dark shades, official-looking badges, and carrying guns. As they came into the main waiting area, they walked toward the podium where my girls were. I wondered what they were doing. Chuckling to myself I uttered under my breath, "I hope they did not see my stash of drugs (medicines), surgical supplies, and twenty plus Parkie the Raccoon stuffed animals. Nothing suspicious here." My imagination was running wild with crazy scenarios when I suddenly heard my name called over the intercom.

I stood to attention stiffer than I already was. "I hope they don't think I am smuggling drugs," I mumbled under my breath thinking of the stuff in my suitcase I had just been laughing about.

My husband turning to face me asked, "What did you do now?"

I shrugged my shoulders, stepping out of line as I displayed my passport to the agent at the counter. I crossed the divide toward where my girls were standing. As I got closer to the podium, they just stared at me, wondering why I was called. When I got to where the airline desk agent was standing, I realized that my husband had left the other line and was close on my heels, wondering what trouble I had gotten myself into this time.

Still shaking my head at the girls' lack of apparent concern for whatever was happening or about to happen, the in-flight security officers passed me and my husband without uttering a word and proceeded nonchalantly toward the jetway. I realized that one of the officers kept staring at me which only made me more nervous so there went the waterworks again. I got my fan out trying to gently fan myself like a lady but that was not helping so my fanning got more vigorous, and my hair began to feel as if I had just stepped out of the shower. But I could not go refresh because the airline desk agent had not told me the problem yet.

Ten minutes had passed, and still I was no closer to understanding why I was singled out. My appearance was that of a mad woman by now: mascara running down my cheeks, hair dripping, back soaking wet and huge sweat stains under my bosom. Finally, after the entire plane was boarded, the airline desk agent comes and asks if I can switch seats with another passenger. Really? That was the question?

My imagination had run wild, and now I needed a shower and a complete set of fresh dry clothes. After all that undue stress and imagination going wild, we ended up with better seats. At least once settled I could wash up and change but that's another story trying to maneuver in a small, confined space while stiff and slow but after struggling for a while I got comfy and dry. I like it when a plan comes together!

Going back a few years, I remember we were worried I had a new, potentially more malignant cancer than the melanomas and thyroid cancer I had before. So, after waiting all summer in agony to find out if I had yet another type of cancer or metastatic disease from one of my previous cancers, the day finally came to go to MD Anderson. I was especially apprehensive and scared. First, I never looked good or did well early in the morning, especially if I have not slept. Second, seeing the reaction of my husband and our friend (who is also a radiologist) to this big mass in my liver I was almost certain the findings would not be good. My husband was hovering over me, stroking me, and holding my hand because he, too, was terrified. Plus, he was trying to keep himself calm more than me while helping me answer questions since my PD med was not fully on yet.

During the admission intake, the nurse suddenly looked over at my spouse and asked him to step outside. I said there was no need, there were no secrets, we were here to find out if I had cancer and I felt better with him in the room. She disregarded my comments, leaned in very close almost whispering and continued her admission report.

As a doctor, and as a patient who has been through many tests and surgeries, I know the routine. Diagnosis, medications, surgeries, allergies, family history, etc. Suddenly, she began asking me questions pertaining to human trafficking. She asked if I was being held against my will. I was lying there half asleep, half dreading a biopsy, and I suddenly snaped back thinking I had misunderstood the question.

Sensing my trepidation and confusion at the question, she touched my hand and told me not to worry, that he couldn't hear us.

"What?" I asked. Obviously, this was not just a general inquiry or awareness campaign. She thought I was in danger and being held captive for whatever reason. "Of course not," I said. "That's my husband. Could you please tell him to come back," and I called out for him. He heard me and walked back into the room. Upon seeing him approaching the bed to hold my hand, she kicked him out again.

Then I got really upset, both at her for testing my already frail nerves and at him for not protesting this nonsense. Here I was having a horrible day already; I surely did not need this. I had worked at MD Anderson for a few years in the past and didn't recall this line of questioning during admission intake. Nor at any other hospital or facility I had worked at.

Finally, she was done. My husband was allowed back in the room. Before the biopsy, I needed to have some preliminary tests. So, I went to the bathroom to give a urine sample and there I saw the bathroom stalls were plastered with posters about human trafficking. At the time, I was a nervous wreck and made more upset by the line of questioning and nurse's apparent insensitivity to my feelings. I was in total disbelief for what I had just undergone as if the idea of having cancer was not stressful enough.

This incident reminded me how important it is to have a caregiver if we are not able to speak for ourselves about the symptoms of Parkinson's in the off stage. I may look apprehensive, anxious, have difficulty speaking and may even have bruises and abrasions if I've fallen.

I don't go out much these days as trouble has a way of finding me, so I try to stay low key. But sometimes even in my own home there is excitement.

Once, I opened my front door to go out to run an errand, and I suddenly was bombarded with a slew of police officers with K9s. They were combing my front lawn and backyard.

"Now what?" I murmured to myself.

I heard an officer yell, "Ma'am, please go back inside."

I asked what was going on and got no response. I was not going to hang out there and find out, so I quickly turned around and went inside but not before glancing up and down the street. The whole neighborhood was covered with K-9 units, police and a slew of unmarked cars lined the street.

Apparently, there was an escaped convict who had entered one of the neighbors' homes. Fortunately, no one was injured.

As you can see, trouble has a way of finding me. Never a dull moment whether I stay on my couch at home or decide to venture out. And I never go out in the early morning because as my chairman, the late Dr. Calverley always said, "Nothing good ever happens before 9:00 a.m." Words to live by.

Needless to say, I forgot the principle of avoiding trouble at all costs . . . and that nothing good ever happens before 9:00 a.m. I decided to venture to the grocery store early one morning to start the day. Well, I assure you that was the last time I ever will go against my own principles and beliefs. The result of not listening to yourself can be dangerous—I walked into an armed robbery. So, there you have it.

Thank God for DoorDash—I can avoid car crashes, police shoot-outs, armed robberies and being boxed in the parking lot by the cars parked on adjacent sides. Once, finding myself in this situation and unable to find the owners of the trucks (this is Texas, after all) I attempted to crawl from the back into the driver's seat. Well, I can tell you this was not a brilliant idea. Having Parkinson's caused me to get stuck between the rows and I just laid there for a while until eventually one truck moved and I could exit the back row. But of course, it would have been nice if it was the passenger's side that became free. No such luck, and I was stuck again straddling that console in the middle of the car unable to get into the driver's seat. After I don't know how many minutes passed before I finally climbed behind the steering wheel and took off. This is when I decided I needed to do a lot more stretching exercises and always park far away from people.

After finally overcoming the fear of getting the COVID-19 virus after the pandemic —because I am like a magnet for viruses, bacteria etc., it is as if they are waiting for me to step outside to invade me—I almost feel like I need to be in a bubble to go out. I am not kidding. The last two years have been the worst and each time I catch something it put me down for months at a time. So, I went back to my pulmonologist to find the cause. I know he did not believe me when I said how frequently I was getting sick until I kept showing up in his office sick. And after the third time in a row, he said, "I can't believe you are sick again." I felt as if I was discovering a new world. Strange and odd, yet exciting.

No matter how long I remain in seclusion my outings always culminate with a crazy, bizarre, or silly story to recount, which in a way makes living with a myriad of diseases a lot more interesting. Otherwise, I would not have any material to write about.

My latest misadventure nearly landed me in jail but could have gotten me killed had I been off my dopamine. When I am off or in severe pain, I tend to have little if any filters when I speak—thank you, Parkinson's. Then I probably would have made headlines portrayed as a hostile and uncooperative Hispanic woman who threatened an officer. Thank goodness I was fully medicated with high levels of dopamine in my system.

The truth is, I have survived much worse. Many years ago, when my grandparents were still alive, we used to make frequent trips to Mexico to visit them and, for whatever reason, my family always loved to travel under the cloak of night through the most deserted roads. My obsession with always having a full tank of gas comes from being traumatized more than once during these trips when invariably we would run out of gas because Dad missed the last gas station for miles. On one particular trip during Christmas season, halfway between San Antonio and the border we ran out of gas. It was very cold and foggy. My dad left my family in search of gas around 3:00 a.m. walking into the fog. We did not see him again until about 10:00 a.m. It was one of the scariest nights of my life as if taken out of one of

Stephen King's novels. Because of the fog, we could not see anything outside our window. All we were left with was the sound of coyotes howling in the distance. At times, the sounds seemed like they were coming from right outside our car. I think that if someone had jiggled the door handle, I would have fainted. We did not know if our dad had been mauled by a wild animal, kidnapped, run down or what? My brother and sister were too young and just slept through everything but me being the eldest, helped mom keep guard with a stiff lip. Although, I just wanted to cry. Instead of worrying, which was my natural tendency, I learned to replace worrying and fear by singing and praying. It has worked thus far. This helped strengthened my belief in God.

Finally, another memorable trip to visit my grandparents occurred about a year before they passed away. When my grandfather took ill requiring hospitalization for the first time in eighty-two years, we knew this was serious. Since my grandfather was the world to me, I knew I had to travel to see him. All the men were tied up, so it was only mom and me. Why on earth did I let her convince me to travel at night after all the scary experiences we had growing up? God only knows. I guess the idea was to arrive at the crack of dawn to not waste the day.

So, there we were, having crossed the border, and instead of waiting for daylight, my mother insisted we continue through the night. This was before the main highway was completed, which meant all the old back roads were desolate and pitch black. We had just passed a small town and had made a turn onto old Highway 57, when an unmarked car came out of nowhere and began following us. I thought about making a run for it, but there was really no place to run to. Plus, I am not sure my little Mazda would *zoom, zoom* as the advertisements suggested.

When in doubt, call on a higher power. My mother and I held hands and began to pray. By now they had caught up to us, and I had no choice but to stop at the only dim streetlamp I saw. Four men exited the car carrying machine guns. The praying had calmed me, but it was not hard to imagine what the headlines would be if this went south. Trying to stay calm as the men in black military-style clothing approached my car, Mom and I continued praying. Me in silence because I'd lost my breath at thought of what was about to transpire. My mom somehow found the strength to pray louder. They surrounded the car. I thought I had locked the doors. I was petrified when one of the men opened the passenger door. He pointed an assault rifle at my mother's rib cage. She remained perfectly calm as I noticed a fifth man getting out of the vehicle. When he reached us, he settled the others who had begun to make lewd comments and harass us. He then began asking us questions in a conversationally polite manner. Before we knew it, we had been released to go on our way and all it cost us was a good scare, $100, and some tacos. God is good. But I didn't stop shaking until we got to my grandfather's, and that was the last time I drove into Mexico at night or without a male companion.

I know I am notorious, but sometimes my life reads like a movie often reminding me of the movie *Big Fish*, in which the father and son relationship is estranged because the protagonist gets tired of his father's exaggerated stories only to discover they were all true. I guess my friends and patients were correct when they said troublemaker was my middle name.

But the real takeaway message here is that no matter how much trouble there is around us or we get ourselves into, there is a higher power, a God that cares about us and is there to guide us and protect us even in the darkest hours. Whether it be a chronic progressive illness like Parkinson's disease, an emotional, physical, or mental trauma, or even the loss of a loved one, if we simply call on HIM, he will comfort us. All my many mishaps have taught me to confide in God and depend on His mercy and grace. These tough situations have made me enjoy even the smallest of victories. I have mastered the skill of reaping the benefits of life's peaks and not taking anything for granted. So come what may, I know there is hope and I am secure (Job 11:18, Jeremiah 29:11).

CHAPTER 14

Brain Fog

"It is not the clear-sighted who rule the world. Great achievements are accomplished in a blessed, warm mental fog."

— *Joseph Conrad*

I love that car insurance commercial that says we all have those days, then proceeds to show all the crazy things people do. Well, I am not sure if I can attribute all my debacles to PD, but it seems like I do more stupid things now than I ever did before.

P.J. O'Rourke quipped, "If we're looking for the source of our troubles, we shouldn't test people for drugs, we should test them for stupidity..." Well, to this I say that it is not really ignorance or lack of intelligence, but rather foolish behavior caused by uncooperating brain cells who simply decided to take their sweet time in responding or not show up at all when needed. My neurons surely run like molasses which I blame solely on the Parkinson's. The longer I live with this disease the slower I become from head to toe. Everything is *taka, taka, taka* like the gearwheel or cogwheel of a watch rotating ever so slowly to mesh with the teeth of a comparable part just as it loses its power and comes to a complete halt. All the information and parts are there to perform their duties to perfection, but it requires an external force to maintain motion.

Levodopa is my key to all movement, whether it is connecting one brain neuron to another or simply moving a limb. However, as the disease has progressed, I have developed so many side effects with levodopa that it's hard to maintain the right amount needed to maintain the rapid firing connections to maximize my neuronal activities. At times, these connections just don't seem to want to do their job, and they seem to go nowhere fast. Hence, I do and say the most absurd things.

Okay, granted, I have always been a rare bird. For one, I have never been good at adages or proverbs. I usually get them mixed up. So, I must remind my doctors and family that this is not a sign of senility nor is my poor penmanship or horrible construction abilities. Of course, those who just meet me, at first glance may wonder how on earth I ever became a doctor. God only knows. I wonder that myself, on occasion, when I am off levodopa, and I am incapable of carrying out simple addition and subtraction. Sometimes trying to leave a tip is as complex a task as trying to solve an advanced mathematical equation. Funny, because I was pretty good at math once upon a time.

I often say the darndest things when I am in a brain fog, so much so that my husband along with my nephew and daughter have a running list of all the crazy, bizarre things I say and do when I am in this state of mind. Granted, I have been living with PD for seventeen years, so you can imagine the list is quite long. However, it seems that over the last couple of years, this list has fueled an interest among my family members. My nephew lived with us for a while and began keeping his own list, and once they found out each had a list, the competition began, and eventually my daughter got involved in chronicling the "Bebe Follies."

My frequent one-liners have become a hit on holidays. This past Christmas, everyone was comparing their lists and recommended that for next year everyone come up with the two best sayings for each month to be voted on at the end of the year to determine the winning remark. I think it's hilarious. My husband is so attached to the list that he has made it clear he wants to be buried with it, and on a recent visit with my daughter, the first thing she asked her dad was to see the silly and crazy list.

As of late, the list keeps growing by leaps and bounds because when I am fully on, I tend to get manic and act over the top sometimes. For instance, the other day my husband asked me why I had so many cups in front of me at the coffee table. I said I was drinking from all of them.

"All of them?" he reiterated.

And I proceeded to point out what each one was for, carefully. Touching each cup as I went along ... coffee, coffee, coke, tea.

"Why two coffee drinks?" he inquired.

"One is cold, and the other is hot," I said, smiling.

The thing is that as of late, I am not hungry, but I crave cold drinks. So usually, I keep various types of beverages on hand. Sometimes I want a new drink before finishing the one I have. Instead of putting the unfinished one away like normal people would do, I simply get a new drink and begin a collection of drinks and throughout the day I add more ice when I want to go back to a drink unless it has become so watered down or no longer tastes good because it lost its fizz, etc. Maybe this is my newfound OCD (obsessive-compulsive disorder) to go along with my Candy Crush obsession and watching shows I enjoy over and over when dopamine is low. I guess it is better than the alternatives. Miraculously my need for caffeinated drinks, crushing away and watching re-runs disappears with an increase in levodopa without altering my dopamine agonists.

At other times, I don't know which way is up. I dare not leave the house during these times. When my brain decides not to join in, anything can and will happen. Some instances cause me to just shake my head, pondering how many neurologists would it take to do whatever it is that I have done or failed to do. Other times, my antics simply make me laugh out loud. Like the time I walked out without a shirt wearing only my red *brassiere* and jacket. It reminded me of the scene from an old TV show where woman caused accident because everyone stopped to stare. Fortunately, that has not occurred. You've heard that old saying - if I didn't have bad luck, I would have no luck at all. Well, that's the way I feel sometimes. I don't cause it, but I always seem to find its lair along my path.

Back in 2017, when the name Maria was chosen as a potential hurricane name my friends all went on alert. They knew for sure it would become a storm and be a bad one. Sure enough, my friends' predictions came true. Hurricane Maria went down in history as a Category 5 hurricane which devastated the island of Puerto Rico.

My family is so used to my shenanigans that they seem to have accepted it's just part of my personality.

Another time, early on in my disease, I was having so much trouble with my medications that I was walking like a zombie most of the time. One day, I stopped to check my mailbox, and I simply got out of the car without putting it in parking mode. My car started rolling downhill. Fortunately, it did not go very far, and no one was injured. It's amazing how adrenaline kicks in and I could move quickly when only a few minutes before I was hobbling out and getting stuck on the seat belt.

My worst embarrassment that ever occurred was at a doctors' Christmas party. I wish the earth could have swallowed me whole right then and there. I had not seen many of my colleagues, so I was excited, greeting everyone and everyone seemed happy to see me again after a long hiatus. However, it would have been best if I had never attended. As a matter of fact, I don't think I ever got the nerve to show up again to another doctors' party after that night. There I was in full Maria mode, as my friends call it. I was having a grand old time and did not notice that my medication had worn off when I made the worse *faux pas* of my life asking someone where their wife was when she was standing next to him because I had him confused with another person. The worse part again is that lack of filter I keep mentioning. When he said this is my wife instead of saying something like, "Oh I am sorry I did not recognize you," like normal people would do, I looked at her and then looked at him with bewilderment. *Did he get divorced?* I thought to myself.

Due to my prosopagnosia (poor face recognition) which I experienced early on in the disease, I often was very disconcerted. Not recognizing who he was and mistaking him for my neighbor whose wife I knew well, I blurted out, "That's not your wife! Where is Dr so and so?" Well, you can imagine how well that went. I wish the earth had opened up at that instant when I realized my mistake and swallowed me whole. Any sane, rational person with a full deck of cards would have realized their mistake and attempted to apologize. Even if I had not been so bewildered by the whole incident and thought logically afterwards, there simply was no coming back from that. I still feel awful when I think of that scenario. I imagine this is what it must be like for people when getting dementia. Fortunately, I am not there yet. And will never be there. I am certain there was lots of talk after I left. Probably being thankful I was no longer practicing.

Then there was the infamous mailbox mishap at my daughter's friend's mom's house. Ever since being diagnosed with Parkinson's, I have had a hard time backing up my car. I go extremely slow. For whatever reason, my brain was not firing on all cylinders and instead of pressing on the brake as I went in reverse, I pressed on the gas. The car veered to the side and hit the mailbox. That is probably my second most embarrassing moment, especially for my daughter. You can imagine she did not want me to drive her anywhere for a long time.

Lately, it seems that sometimes no matter how hard I try to make things better the more complicated they get thanks to my brain fog. This unfortunately is the result of living with multiple illnesses that affect my brain, making it sluggish and inattentive at times especially under duress. Even my mother, who has early dementia, has been flabbergasted by my so-called good will interventions which have only served to muddle the waters. But really, I am the only one that suffers the consequences plus I have to backtrack to fix whatever problem I'd created.

Not long ago, Mom had been having trouble handling her finances. Of course, as a good daughter and caregiver, I offered to take over some of her finances to ease her burden. Sadly, the only time she had any trouble resulting in interruption of her utilities was when I got involved. I suppose it is true what they say, no good deed ever goes unpunished. Guess who had to pay all the fines? You guessed it, me! My husband pokes fun at me at the fact that the only time my mother was inconvenienced and distraught was under my helm. Well, so much for me being mentally competent. At least my daughter knows how to ascertain my state of mind any time there are important issues to discuss.

Some days when the fog sets in, especially when my lupus and migraines are acting up on top of my Parkinson's, I could very well lose my head if it were not attached. In my defense, the water utility bill not being paid was a complete oversight. My credit card got hacked when I traveled to Miami to install my daughter for her summer internship. As a matter of fact, my entire family's credit cards and debit cards were compromised. In the credit card chaos, traveling, and ensuring we had cash, I completely forgot about my mother until I got the call. Her meter had been padlocked, and she had no water. Making matters worse, I got to hear from everyone about my negligence in taking care of Mom, even though I was the one that suffered the embarrassment as well as the penalty fees and dealing with the company in trying to restore services ASAP for her.

The second time was more of a funny incident brought on again by feeling pressured and stressed when having a flare-up and everyone making demands on me. Mom was staying with me, and she remembered she had not made a particular payment and needed me to take care of it. However, she has an uncanny way of asking for my assistance with things at the times when I am feeling most rundown. She was upset because the payment was going to be late. I attempted to pay online but I couldn't log in, nor verify the information because she was not home. You know how that goes. I probably spent close to an hour trying to make the payment. It would have been nice to pay by phone, but no such luck. I think this is one of the biggest problems we have nowadays, making it more difficult for the elderly, especially those who are not tech savvy or are cognitively compromised to be able to live independently. God help us all when my mind starts to slip. I tell you it is hard keeping up with my stuff, my mother's, and my husband's. I need those paper bill reminders otherwise I would lose track of things much more easily. I had to cancel some credit cards because they wanted to charge a fee for a paper bill. I need the redundancy to be able to function at times.

Since I was unsuccessful, I simply wrote a check and went to the post office to expedite delivery. Unfortunately, with the added confusion, I mailed it back to her home. A week later when I dropped her off at her house and I retrieved her mail l saw the envelope with my return label among her other bills. At first, I was puzzled, then realized what had happened. Of course, now she would get a late fee. Fortunately, they knew her well at the bank, and they were able to dismiss the late charges. Now I have to triple check all my outgoing mail and have my husband give it a once over before mailing just in case. Plus, I have set up electronic and paper bills as backup for me and my mother to avoid future mishaps. Funny thing, Mom is the one with memory trouble, yet she knows exactly when each bill is due. I guess that's what you call selective memory. Me, on the other hand, my memory bank in these matters is divided by time of the month - beginning, middle and end.

However, the funniest and somewhat embarrassing incident I endured thanks to my poor motor skills was the humiliation of not having my cake bought at an auction sale. I can't blame my Parkinson's entirely but had a lot to do with it. This was a classic Maria award-winning *Nailed It!* moment. For those of you who do not know about *Nailed It!*, a TV show . . . this is a program in which people with poor kitchen skills seek redemption by trying to recreate edible masterpieces. My nephew, who should have been a gourmet chef, introduced me and my family to this show. They all agree that I should have entered. (The show is no longer airing.) They were convinced I would have had a good chance to win because my problem is not cooking, but rather, executing a visually tasty product when it comes to baked goods. It is a well-kept secret in my family that I am a good cook. The thing is that everyone in my family loves to cook and spend time in the kitchen, so I always defer especially now as my Parkinson's has progressed. I enjoy creating and making meals for holidays especially. However, because of all my medical issues, I am very selective as to when I cook and for whom. Although, I am always relegated to clean-up duties when family is around— which I think is so much harder—but since I don't have a deadline to meet, I acquiesce to cleaning. However, I finally bought nice dishes which are dishwasher machine friendly to help me out with the task. Plus, sometimes the repetitive motion of cleaning so many pots and pans can trigger my dystonia, making it difficult to wash dishes properly.

Keeping this in mind, my self-esteem suffered a low blow one Thanksgiving during a fund raiser event. As a Pilot Club International member (an international club founded in Macon, Georgia, on October 18, 1921, by women leaders of the community to provide service and foster friendship among women) we performed lots of service activities for the community. We did things like providing meals to the patients with Alzheimer's and Parkinson's and other elderly patients at adult day cares in town and senior centers. They also provided money and other supplies for patients with traumatic brain injuries as well as providing tracking bracelets for elderly patients with dementia. The service to people with neurological disease was one of the main reasons I joined. However, because of the money required to do all these activities, we often had fundraisers.

Serving and cooking was a lot of work, but it was also very rewarding, especially during the Valentine's dinner and autumn festivities for the special need kids and adults. However, after the last fundraising bake sale, I was so saddened that my husband convinced me to quit. I think this is the only time I have ever quit in my life. I attempted to go back several times but having two major illnesses has made me entirely unreliable for most scheduled activities, especially when a weekly commitment is required.

This unpredictability of symptoms has been one of the biggest issues I have had to deal with and despite nearly two decades I can't seem to get used to it. I was the most reliable person—if I committed to something or said I would do something, you knew it would be done come hell or high water. Now it is a struggle, but I don't give up trying to volunteer and stay active in my community. Although I stay active as much as my body can tolerate, there are things I miss like singing in the choir and working with women in ministry.

During my last fundraiser event everyone was asked to bring two cakes to auction as a means of fundraising. Of course, being the holidays, I wanted something extra special. I wanted my cakes to be auctioned for a higher bid to help the organization help more individuals. Never did I imagine that making two appealing-to-the-eye cakes would be such an ordeal. I was in over my head. I ended up making ten cakes, because each attempt at decorating the cake resulted in a terrible disaster. Of course, as the night went on my motor skills only worsened due to my dystonia. The constant mixing did not help. I could not decorate a single cake that was presentable in my eyes to save my life. I tried all types of frosting and decorations including fruits, flowers, nuts, and powdered sugar. They were all pitiful.

The best-looking one was the Bundt cake dusted with plain powdered sugar, which was the one I ended up taking. The numerous cakes sitting on my kitchen island smelled delicious but looked unappealing. I wanted to cry from frustration and outright fatigue from baking for at least six hours straight without a good outcome. When I moved the last one, I pushed way too hard in frustration, and it split in half which just made me laugh. I took a bite, and I was pleased with the taste. My grandmother, who was a great confectioner, would have been pleased with the taste and consistency. Yet, I doubted anyone would be willing to try it given its current state. So, I did the next best thing, I went and bought a cake at the bakery at the last minute to serve as one of the two. At least this one was presentable, although I was certain it did not meet the taste standard. It reminded me of why we should never judge a book by its cover or a person by their outer appearance. When the auction began, all the cakes were selling for $50 and up, but my poor little Bundt cake only got $10. I think the gentleman who bought it felt sorry for me.

When my nephew first saw the collection of cakes on my counter when he entered the kitchen upon his arrival, he said, "What happened here?" and started laughing. I told him what happened and my disappointment at the looks of disapproval I had received. My daughter and nephew, however, cheered me up by saying that whoever had bought the Bundt cake probably had gotten a surprise once they tasted it. Plus, it only cost ten bucks. Of course, it took them a while to stop laughing at my funky cake collection. Their laughter was so contagious that I joined in with them and came up with an idea to open an "ugly cake" bakery just for the holidays. To this day, my family still talks about the worst-looking, best-tasting butter cake with chocolate and almonds. That Thanksgiving, there was no shortage of desserts, and not a morsel was left afterward.

The thing I have discovered is that there is no fog too dense that the light of God cannot penetrate. In all these years of being in a fog I have lost some things like abilities, friends, my career and perhaps a bit of sanity but have found a new beginning, new friends, new purpose, new skills and career, and most importantly, I have found myself. I discovered I possessed a strong inner light within my soul which I now try to spread to all those around me. So, for those of you who are still wandering out in the fog, not sure where to go, there is a safe lighthouse waiting for you just beyond the mist. He sees our heart and not anything else. Some of us are purple jade, while others may be amethyst or red quartz. Don't fret about what you may look like on the outside; it is what's inside that give us our worth.

CHAPTER 15

Beans and Rice

"He demands acceptance on his own terms."
— Lloyd Alexander

Thereis a Mexican saying that everything resembles its owner. Nothing is truer than this. In fact, many studies have shown that our feline friends pick up on and adopt our own personalities. So, if your feline is less than social, well I am afraid there is no one else to blame. My big baby whose name is Binx is also known as Beans or *Frijolito* by my Mexican friends and family. Spending any time with him would reveal that he has my own finicky personality. He is delicate and temperamental. And of course, as all felines do, he loves to sleep during the day. This is the perfect pet for me since both of us sleep in the day (for me it is most of the morning since I typically don't go to bed until 3:00 a.m.).

Binx and I are most alert and energized at night. We have a very narrow window of comfort, and any minor alterations can throw us for a loop. Stress, even so-called good stress, can cause me to have a lupus flare-up which I absolutely hate, so I try to pray and spend time doing things that nourish my mind and soul in a quiet, cool place with not very much light—although most of my family members hate that I often keep my house darker than they would prefer. Nothing worse than waking up struggling, stumbling, foggy brained, and then blinded by bright light. I must be partly vampire because I swear there are times when I not only cringe at the light but make hissing noises and start closing all the shades quickly before I melt. My feline friend also has a small window in which he thrives. He, too, hates noises, and too many visitors stress him out at times causing him to get ulcers as well like

I do. We are a hot mess often traveling full speed on the hot mess express lane. He truly is my protector and companion. Glad my girls got him. I like having a cat to look after and talk to as well. However, if he starts talking back, we will have a problem.

When he was just a kitten, he imitated my movements or lack there off which was hysterical. When I had trouble ambulating, dragging my leg, so did he. One day I was hurting so much and experiencing leg weakness that I could not even stand up and take a few steps so, I crawled around my home propelling myself with my upper body. A day or so later, I caught a glimpse of my furry friend trailing behind me imitating all my moves dragging his two little hind legs. My heart melted and tears trickled down my cheeks at the site of this. I grabbed him and put him on my shoulder, and I managed to get both of us into the bedroom where we remained for several days. He stayed by my side unable to use his hind legs until I was able to get up and walk normally. After a show of solidarity and affection of this magnitude how can one not love such a feline? I had become his mother. Since I have many allergies to domestic animals, and somehow my other pets as a child always ended up being a meal it was incredibly hard to build a strong lasting rapport with any one creature. Nevertheless, I love animals, especially when young. My grandfather often raised chickens, rabbits, and goats. I especially loved feeding the baby goats. When I was a teenager, that's when I discovered the severity of my allergies to cats and dogs.

After all these years of avoiding having a pet, I am delighted to have such a special companion. I am so protective of him, typical mother behavior. I swear he makes a vocalizing sound that mimics the word *mama*. They say cats only use verbal cues with humans to have them do what they need. Well, it must be true because he only utters this sound when he is trying to get my attention after he has been neglected because I was sick or out of town. He also verbalizes this particular word in a rapid succession, and it becomes louder and louder when he is excited or when he sees me getting his favorite treats.

Over the years, he has become more in tune with my up and down cycles. When I am sick, he does not leave my side. During these times, the frequency and intensity of his purring increases, as if he were trying to comfort me and send healing vibes. Some say that these purring sounds are indeed curative.

When I travel, I don't like to leave him with anyone other than my mom. This is because he gets very stressed and won't eat and depending on how stressed he gets he will then develop ulcers. Prior to my sister coming to live with my mom he felt at home at her house and had his own special room. However, my sister's arrival and taking over his special room made him quite unhappy. He, like my daughter, does not jump into new situations right away. It takes them both some time to develop bonds and get used to the new environment. So, no more staying at Grandma's, at least for a while.

During the last trip, I found him hiding behind the curtains and would not come out until he saw my face. The entire way home he sat there looking pitiful until we got to our neighborhood. I suppose that since cats have a highly developed sense of smell, he might have suddenly recognized some familiar scents when we lowered the window as we drove down our street. Suddenly, he stood up, changing his demeanor and began looking out the window with excitement. As we entered the driveway to our home, it was as if he recognized this was home. I swear he began wagging his tail (did not know cats wag their tails but they do) and could not wait to be let out. When we opened the door of the van, he jumped out and went to the house door waiting to be let in.

Once inside the house, he ran around inspecting all his favorite places. When this was completed, he just threw himself stretching and rolling around on the cool marble floor of the entryway. He knew this was home and he was ecstatic. He immediately began to purr and show me his belly so that I could rub it. This canine-like behavior reminded me of *Skippyjon Jones,* the story of the little Siamese cat who thinks he is a Chihuahua. Just like Chihuahuas, my big kitty has a feisty personality and is very protective of me, my husband and daughter. He, too, has a strong attachment and suffers separation anxiety when I am gone even if leave him alone with my spouse. And boy will he let me know his displeasure upon my return. He comes over to me when I arrive home and begins mouthing a lot, as if giving me a long list of complaints. After these separations, if I try to get near him or stroke him, he evades me and turns his head away in disdain. A bit like my daughter when she was a child. A few hours later, he starts to come over and press himself against my leg, but I still cannot touch him until he is ready to be stroked. My child was the same way; I could not initiate contact unless she initiated it first. She would press her head on my chest and snuggle up against me, and then I could wrap my arms around her. It had to be on her own terms. No wonder I think we are part feline. We have the surname to prove it.

My baby Maw-maw, as I call him, and I usually have a good time playing hide-and-seek, mostly in the wee hours of the night. Although half of the time, you can see his tail sticking out. I pretend not to see him and walk away so he peeps until his eyes meet mine, then he runs to hide somewhere else. He just loves being chased all over the house, just as my daughter did as a toddler. Since he can't speak and ask to be chased, he simply grabs my leg when he is ready for playtime. All I have to say is, "I am coming to get you," in either Spanish or English, and he jumps with excitement and begins running.

The pantry is one of his favorite places to hide. The pantry has been the favorite room in the house for of all my nieces, nephews, and my daughter's friends, even now when everyone is an adult. The last time a friend came over for the holidays, the first thing she did after saying hello was walk to the pantry, looking for a particular soda pop I often kept. It still tickles me. It is also the last stop on the way out to get a treat for the road. Binx loves this room, too. He likes to hide behind and inside the soda boxes as well as inside the paper bags.

Once, he was so frantically trying to hide from me that he jumped into a soda box which was still half full. Thus, when he jumped into the box he punctured a soda can. This caused a huge hissing sound and a sudden explosion that looked like a geyser had erupted. The sound and wetness caused him to sprint out jumping at least a foot off the ground. I laughed so hard at the sight of him dripping wet all over with sticky lids and paws. I wish I had had a video camera. I think it would have been a good entry for *America's Funniest Home Videos*.

This incident reminds me of the time I accidentally left a can of sprite in my car—in the sun—while I saw patients in the office. When I got in the car, I was suddenly stuck to the seat, foot pedals, steering wheel. I saw the can of soda, but it was closed until I picked it up and realized it was empty. There was only a tiny pinhole on one side, where the pressure had built up until it found a way out—toward the driver's side of course.

Cleaning the pantry was almost as much fun as cleaning my car. Binx loves the pantry still but no longer jumps into soda boxes or any other open box.

My sweet daughter's favorite game as a toddler besides being chased was hide-and-seek, and unlike my *Frijolito*, she was much more difficult to find. She could hide well for hours and being so tiny she fit almost anywhere. Once, she gave me quite a scare—she'd hidden inside one of the cabinets and fell asleep. Thank goodness she was smart enough to leave a small crack for air to circulate. Otherwise, I hate to think what would have happened.

My husband treats Binx like our baby. Although now he is a big cat and is more difficult to carry around, my husband still enjoys this time with him. When we brought Binx home, he was so tiny he used to fit in the palm of his hand just as our daughter did, being only four pounds at birth. It is funny to see him chasing Maw-maw and playing with him like he used to with our daughter. When *Frijolito* was a kitten, my husband would carry him in his arms, rocking him while talking to him and showing him things around the home. Same way he used to do with our daughter.

Binx was just as fascinated with this activity as my child once was. Since we could not have any more children, I suppose this little furry friend filled that void for both of us. Although, after eight years, he is not as interested in being held or carried around as before. Plus, he is now a big cat that is hard to lift up for long periods of time. Yet, he is as agile as the day he was born. He runs fast, especially up the stairs. However, he knows when I am having a slow day. During these days, when I chase him, he slows down his pace sometimes to a crawl so that I may be able to catch up to him.

My brother has adopted a cute beige Chihuahua. Although Monty (Montezuma) has been part of the family for a long time now, he just won't accept me. All it takes is one glimpse of me and he goes berserk. Barking and running around me trying to contain me. The interesting part is that even the slightest perception of my voice, even over the phone, causes him to stir from sleep and begin barking incessantly. It is hysterically funny to watch. You would think that since all the other members of the family are also cat owners, he would give them the same treatment, but this is not the case. I suppose it goes along with me being "special." No amount of caressing, cooing, or bribing with treats has made him let his guard down when I am around. The only explanation that I have is that he is jealous and protective of my brother. My brother and I have always had a deep connection, which we call ESN (extra special nerdiness). We think a lot alike and love many of the same things.

Joseph Krutch wrote that, "Cats seem to go along on the principle that it never does any harm to ask for what you want." I certainly hold on to this philosophy. I believe we would be so much happier if we were truthful with ourselves in what we really want and need. This way we would stop wasting our energy on fruitless ventures and instead pursue those things which would bring us joy and comfort. I don't know of anyone else other than babies who can get, ". . .food without labor, shelter without confinement, and love and without penalties" (W. L. George). This is certainly true in Turkey where cats have free reign. Turkey is a cat haven. There they are protected and allowed to roam free. They are loved, played with, and fed by its citizens while the government neuters them to control the population. Perhaps this is because, according to a genetic study of cats, Turkey is one of two birth origins from which all domestic cats are said to come.

In recent years, I have fallen in love with Turkey's culture, which is extremely similar to Hispanic culture and our traditions in so many ways; even the two languages appear to have many similarities. Thus, I would love to spend a summer by the Aegean Sea. However, I am afraid to reach my dream destination only to discover I can't enjoy it due to a potential severe allergic reaction to all the felines roaming the city.

Despite all the hoopla raised by me against adopting a cat, I am happy the majority won, and I got one, nevertheless. This furry ball has become my faithful companion even as I am writing, he is sitting here by my side. He has become an important member of the family so much so that in my official illustration of the Parkinson's Diva logo he is represented and drawn sitting next to me. I am now like all the people I used to laugh at for talking to their pets and treating them like kids. Besides being my companion, he is my guardian as well.

One day in the wee hours of the morning, I felt a small break in my troubles, and I decided to do some writing. I had not been sleeping well caring for my husband who had the flu on top of all the allergic reactions I was experiencing. I ended up with a severe lupus flare-up, not to mention my Parkinson's was in a topsy-turvy state. My head was fuzzy, and I was moving slower than molasses, so everything was taking longer than usual. Why I attempted to write is beyond me.

So, after puttering around for an hour, I realized I was going nowhere. What I needed was rest and sleep. I was running on a minimal dose of dopamine agonist due to severe side effects each time I attempted to take my levodopa. Needless to say, being so under medicated, I was completely off balance and extremely rigid. Finally, I decided to stop wasting time and go to bed before my husband woke up. However, because of my rigidity I struggled to push my chair away from the desk. When I finally unstuck myself from the tight space between the wall and the desk, I still could not get up from the desk chair. I managed to swirl the chair around to give me more room to stand up, but my pen slipped out of my weak hand falling on the floor. Forgetting how stiff and off balance I was, I leaned forward to retrieve it. The moment I put my head down, I knew this was a mistake. I was at the mercy of gravity, being thrust forward faster than I had anticipated due to the heaviness of my head and upper body. With the fatigue, weakness, and complete loss of balance, I toppled over onto the floor into the wastebasket sitting not far from my desk. Fortunately, I did not hit the side table, which was only a few millimeters away from the trash can. I was a helpless ostrich with my head buried and unable to lift my arms to pull the trash basket off or lift my weak neck and head out.

I must have lain there for a few minutes on the floor with my head inside the wastebasket. I did not know if I should laugh or cry, but I was too exhausted to do either. The only comfort and reassurance I got was from my cat which I felt get closer and lay down next to me. A few tears trickled down. Not sure how long I stayed like that before I had enough energy to extricate my head out of the wastebasket. Yet it took another fifteen minutes before I could pull myself up into the chair again, so I could try to stand up from sitting. Meanwhile, my cat continued to lay by my side until I got back on the desk chair. I was in good company with my faithful companion.

When I make *arroz con leche* (rice pudding), he gets excited because he likes condensed milk. Then when the pudding is done, I give him a bit of rice which he licks up so fast. After this event I figured we both needed a sweet treat. Once I was able to extricate myself from the floor and chair, I took a nap with Binx by my side. Having regained some energy after our nap, I made us *arroz con leche*, and we both had seconds.

Things I have learned from my cat which can help us all live better with chronic illnesses:

1. Practice independence,
2. Make sure to take time to nap and reboot your dopamine.
3. Practice self-love by setting proper boundaries. Say *yes* to the things that nourish your soul, your creativity, and your passion, and *no* to the things that drain you and harm you. Remember that even a good thing can be harmful if done to excess.
4. Learn to find balance starting from your spirit outwardly.
5. Be curious. Learn new things. Find new paths.
6. Don't forget to show love and affection. It helps release those naturally good chemicals.
7. Spend time alone. Learn to be comfortable with yourself and spend time praying and meditating.
8. Stay agile. Stretch every day, morning and night—in bed even before you get up or go to sleep.
9. Be flexible in adapting to change; it makes you more resilient.
10. Finally, don't forget to maintain your poise as any diva would do.

CHAPTER 16

Wild-Haired Goddess

"The human hair holds emotional weight the way one's heart does."

— K. Koondhal

Windy days and unruly hair are two of my favorite things. I was born with my grandma's abundantly thick, wavy hair. So thick that each strand was as strong as a guitar string. Ever since I was little, I loved to have my hair brushed by my mom. At a tender age of less than a year, I already had a big personality (subtle way of saying I was a handful). But when you are the first born and first grandchild, people tend to go a bit overboard in the amount of affection they display on you. And when you are a child, sometimes you are unaware of the effect it has on others. Plus, being a bit fragile physically, everyone doted on me, especially my grandfather. Unbeknownst to me, there was a diva in the making. I often asked my mother to brush my hair "in reverse" before going to bed.

Even as a child, I hardly slept during the night. So, someone always had to stay up with me to entertain me with songs, then stories, then books. To this day I love hearing and telling stories, an art I learned from my grandmother. She had a way of keeping you mesmerized as she recounted tales of her youth. At a young age, I discovered the power of storytelling as a way to entertain, communicate information, encourage bonding, and teach lessons to empower the next generation.

When I became a mother, I, too, would tell stories to my daughter as a way of bonding and teaching about our ancestors and for entertainment purposes because she also inherited my severe insomnia. She never slept through the night until she was five years of age. As children, we are always fascinated by discovering self, and many things we learn about the world are through emulation. So, my daughter, too, would recount stories I had told to her dolls as she played with them or brushed their hair.

The cycle was complete when grandma came to live with us at the end of her life and I became her caregiver. Especially since she would get psychotic and confused at times, one way to calm her was to brush her hair which she loved as much as I did as a child. During these times, as I brushed her hair, I would recount stories of when we lived in Mexico, and she would chime in when she recalled certain events. As I groomed her, she would groom my daughter or one of her dolls, whom she mistook as one of the babies she had lost. Interestingly, this simple act always quieted her and brought her back to her full senses. The stories told became part of my daughter's legacy, and she still recalls them.

My curious nature was already beginning to manifest even at such a young age, always wanting to absorb everything in my surroundings. Thus, I insisted on being able to watch myself in the mirror as Mom brushed my hair. Being the only grandchild had its benefits. I was the apple of my grandfather's eye. There was nothing he would not do for me; all I had to do was ask. Our bond remained strong until he passed away. Even now, he remains deep in my heart. He was a Godly man and a very gifted carpenter. Knowing how much I loved to sit and have my hair stroked and brushed while I played with my grandmother's perfumes, lotions, and makeup, he carved for me the prettiest little red chair. He believed in finding just the right type of wood for every project which he tenderly crafted into what spoke to him without ever rushing the process. Although the chair is a bit faded from all the love it has given over the years, it is one of those sentimental objects which has stood the test of time. I have sat in that chair through all the seasons of my life, even when I was pregnant—that is how sturdy it is, not once breaking in half a century. To this day, it is my favorite chair. Although now, on most days, it is hard to use because it is so low to the ground, making it difficult to arise from it. It was also my daughter's favorite chair growing up. My grandfather usually inscribed my name on most things he made for me. So much was my grandfather's love that if he were still alive, he would carve out the name *Parkinson's Diva* on that chair. I am hoping for a fourth-generation Maria with *beaucoup* wild hair to love that little chair . . . and to have her hair groomed as she, too, plays with the perfumes and lotions that belong to her grandmother on the vanity.

My grandfather loved for all the girls of the family to have long hair because he said it accentuated our beauty. He was of the sentiment that a woman's hair is the richest ornament she possesses, just as Martin Luther did. Grandpa always said my hair reminded him of my grandmother's hair when she was young. Since she was the love of his life, having this trait might have unconsciously conferred me extra affection. Of course, this only propelled me further to the center of the universe in my grandfather's eyes. However, I assumed that everyone around me was just as happy as I was.

Because I was mostly raised by my grandparents, my hair was not cut for years. I grew used to having long hair, which I loved, despite the fact that I was never very good at styling it. My grandmother usually would braid it and put ribbons or flowers in it, which is exactly what I did for her when she stayed with me before she passed away.

I never realized that many of the headaches I had growing up were triggered by the heaviness of my hair . . . until I had it cut the last semester of high school. Mom had insisted I get a trim since it was so long, and prom was just around the corner. Rather than a trim, I got all of my hair cut off. I felt a huge loss for the first time. Everyone tried to appease me by saying it would grow back, which did not help—I'd had long hair for almost my entire life. My hair was part of who I was. I felt naked without my long locks. It seemed I had become invisible with my new haircut, adding insult to injury. I was convinced my classmates and teachers did not notice my presence in the classroom due to the absence of my long, flowing hair.

As I became a grown woman, I discovered that I draw much of my strength and confidence from my hair. Of course, it does not confer on me super strength like Samson possessed, but it does give me inner fortitude. Perhaps because it is an outward extension of my personality—wild, bold, and headstrong. I have discovered that the length, style, and texture of one's hair not only conveys a lot about one's feelings, but can shape the attitude of others toward us, as the *Crown Research* study showed.

This study looked at the attitude of employers toward women of color, depending on their hairstyle. Thus, it is not surprising that throughout history, hair has been linked to not only beauty and physical fitness, but also to cultural and spiritual beliefs. For instance, the Tibetan monks shave their head to express their disposal of any material things or ties to this world to seek a higher spiritual state. In other cultures, both men and women cover their hair as part of religious beliefs or religious ceremonies. In ancient Greece, the length of hair was a direct correlation to having a spiritual connection. The longer the hair the wiser and more spiritual the person was believed to be. In the biblical story of Samson, the uncut hair meant a closeness with God. Thus, when he was tricked and his hair cut off, his relationship with the divine was severed, which brought physical weakness. The hair itself did not give the strength; rather, it was God through their intimate relationship, which was based on a pact to not shave his hair.

Although now we don't attribute a person's spirituality or wisdom to hair as in olden times, how we treat our hair remains a window to our deepest inner feelings. This is why it is so important for us as patients, caregivers, and healthcare providers to recognize the importance of the state of a person's hair as an outward manifestation of the inner workings of a person. I have discovered that the first step for emotional, physical, and spiritual well-being to occur is to recognize there is a deficit, embrace it, and then begin to look for answers as to what has caused the damage. The same is true for hair. In other words, spending time grooming, brushing, and taking care of your hair shows self-love. In Parkinson's, self-grooming shows dopamine levels are at their peak. We only have enough drive and energy to spend on making our hair look good when all other basic needs have been met.

After that disastrous first haircut back in high school, I spent years trying to grow my hair and find my own style. Finding a good hairstylist is like finding a good neuro specialist. Not everyone understands the ins and outs of every person's hair needs. Just like not every specialist will understand your unique issues that make your living with Parkinson's or any other disease different than someone else with same illness. I often say, medicine is like any apprenticeship. First, you must learn the fundamental knowledge of the inner workings of whatever it is you are dealing with. However, to be successful and become an expert requires passion and an innate gift. Knowledge is much easier to acquire than mastering the art of how to best apply that mastery.

For years, I searched for stylists to find one who would understand my unique hair challenges. After visiting hundreds of hairstylists all over the country and at all levels, I discovered a handful of people with a gift—true artists and masters in their fields.

This is the same for the field of medicine. There is only a handful of specialists who would understand the unique challenges of your disease and make it all better. However, most physicians will do a respectable job in treating your illness, albeit they may not comprehend all the inner workings of your being. In my case, I believe only God knows how to make me whole. Occasionally, I get glimpses that allow me to continue. It is up to you whether you can live with that outcome or go in search of the few who can do miracles, though it may feel like looking for a needle in a haystack and leave you frustrated. Or do as I do and rely on God to get you through, enhancing your life in the process.

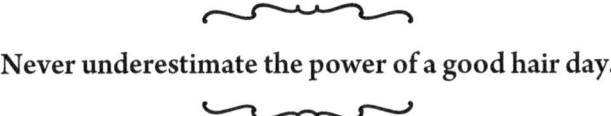

Never underestimate the power of a good hair day.

I feel bolder when my hair is down and unencumbered. Lately, due to the past two years' physical challenges, my hair is screaming for help. I am feeling bound, restrained, slowly losing my zest for life; I feel my wings have been clipped and my independence cut off.

As I mentioned before, our hair conveys as much as our eyes do about our soul and mind—it is a powerful component of a person's individuality and personality. I never fully understood this until I was an adult. My hair is an important part of my Diva identity. I believe my mane is one of my best traits. Unfortunately, as of late, it has relinquished its power of transforming an ordinary day into an extraordinary one—because I had begun to lose my passion for life due to constant battles with my many illnesses. The never-ending rollercoaster of the last two years left me depleted of any zest for much else beyond making it to the next day. These are the times my faith has grown stronger because I had to learn to depend not on my own strength, but on that of a higher power to get me through. The weaker I have become, the stronger He was in showing me His grace and lifting me up. I have learned to accept the things I cannot change.

Either way, I am victorious. If I live and get better, I continue to enjoy my friends and family and do the work I love. If I should get worse and pass away, I will be going home to a better life. This certainty brings forth peace and allows one to focus on crucial matters, like spending time healing without worrying about the future. I am not saying it is easy to do. But thinking of life as seasons helps to not lose hope. After a pruning season, there always comes a flourishing period bearing much fruit. Finally, after a grueling twenty-four months, I seem to finally be getting a handle on all my illnesses, including the new ones I acquired within the last year.

With the fog finally lifting comes a sense of gratitude, along with some trepidation as to what speed I should thrust myself forward. The constant upper respiratory infections had left me emotionally, physically, and mentally devoid of energy and drive, which absolutely reflected in the poor state of my hair. As it is wise to always start at the beginning, the first thing I did was get a new haircut and color to give life back to my hair.

Funny, when you are open to learning and listening to what the universe and God has to say about your life, you find messages in the least likely of places, like a fortune cookie. The fortune stated that my long-standing dream was about to come true. In fact, I got several of them with the same message. After the third or fourth one, I began to ponder about which dream I would be happy to have come true—this book is it! I had been so busy concentrating and living one day at a time, I simply dismissed any long-term goals and dreams, thinking for sure this was the end. But now, I am revitalized . . . with a new hair style to prove it. It was time again to return to my former self—the eternal dreamer and optimist.

Some people feel bolder when they have bright colors in their hair or some other type of intricate style. Just like learning to live with a disease, you must first learn who you are, what you like and do not like. Once you find what makes you happy, feel free to set boundaries for yourself to achieve that happiness. Then you can move on to applying these same principles to your own life and your illness(es). There is freedom and power in embracing your uniqueness. Sometimes you must be fierce and ferocious in all that you do to be victorious.

Today, make sure to take the time to examine your hair status. What it is it saying? If your hair is in shambles, it may be a sign of a deeper underlying problem. If this is the case, other areas of your life could be echoing the same sentiment. Learn to listen to your hair and speak to your health team. Remember healthy, shiny, well-groomed hair is a sign of good self-esteem, inner harmony, and zest for living. Spend some time brushing your hair or, better yet, have your daughter or your grandchild do it for you—take turns, as a form of bonding, and begin your own legacy of storytelling.

CHAPTER 17

Great Expectations

"I looked at the stars, and considered how awful it would be for a man to turn his face up to them as he froze to death, and see no help or pity in all the glittering multitude."

— *Great Expectations* by Charles Dickens

G*reat Expectations* is one of those drawn-out literary masterpieces full of wisdom that I read long ago, but recently, I began to think of some of the passages again when I contemplated the topics for this book—suffering, struggles, challenges, faith, and perseverance. Obstacles and devastating illnesses are what ultimately bind us to each other, making us more compassionate toward one another.

Though out my life journey I have discovered that life is never what you expect. It is full of surprises with many twists and turns and for the most part completely unpredictable. Looking back, if I had to do it over, I would not change a thing despite all the setbacks, and myriads of medical problems which cost me friends along with a thriving career in medicine. However, in return I gained an entire global Parkinson's family. Living with PD also opened the window to a slew of exciting projects, both in the national and international arenas. Plus, it has given me the chance to work with several outstanding organizations, along with renowned scientists and clinicians.

I have had to reinvent myself a few times to keep up with my progressive neurodegenerative disease, learning new skills which, otherwise, I would never have had the opportunity to do. Going through the dark valleys of life, as well as experiencing victories small and big when it all seemed impossible, have molded me into the woman I am today. I have learned that one of the things to keep oneself humble is to have a grateful heart. While character is developed and refined in the valleys, if everything was perfect, there would be no need for faith, nor a God/Savior because we would be able to handle everything on our own. Without trials and tribulations, we would never grow as people nor appreciate the important things which nourish the soul. Faith is based on believing in something, even when you can't see it or touch it. We don't ever question the existence of love or hate, yet we know it is real because we can feel it. The same is true for hope and faith; even though we can't quantify it or hold it in our hand, its mere presence is as vital for our well-being, like the air we breathe. I am much more resilient because of the pain I never saw coming and the physical limitations I have had to endure most of my life, especially since diagnosed with Parkinson's disease and lupus. Throughout my journey, these experiences have expanded my capacity to feel joy, sadness, compassion, and empathy, enriching all my relationships.

Becoming the Parkinson's Diva has been a thrill and an unexpected gift from life and God. However, this never would have happened if one memorable day I had not decided to go to medical school to become a neurosurgeon. This act began to forge the first iron bond in my life, teaching me tenacity, fortitude, and courage. Before it was my friends who supported me, encouraging me to continue following my dream, despite all the naysayers who thought I lacked what it took be a physician. I cannot imagine how different my life would have turned out had those iron bonds not been forged and I had given up on my dream. What if I had never walked into that office in high school and met Maria, who got me a spot at Penn, where I met the professor who fueled the flame for me to become a Parkinson's doctor? Today, there would not be me—a Parkinson's specialist who became a caregiver and a patient advocate.

Over the years, many bonds/relationships have been formed, some weak and some strong, some with thorns and cold as metal, some precious and gentle and fragrant as rose petals. But each served their purpose. Only iron can sharpen iron. While the gentle souls helped me foster kindness and gratitude, each relationship in my past helped to construct my story one bond at a time, like the links of a chain. It is those deep connections and interactions with friends and lovers, some of which remain unbroken throughout the years . . . it is these connections which have given me the courage and strength to keep forging a path wherever it may lead me.

Life is scary at times, but remember . . . courage is the root of change, and change is what we are created for from the minute we are born. Never discard the element of *surprise*—you will be much happier if you accept it and surrender to it. Whether you are a believer that the universe was formed by a seemingly single random event of a single densely hot point that inflated and stretched by some unforeseen force, distributing all matter and energy in all directions with its explosion (Big Bang Theory), or that a God created everything by uttering a word to make it come into existence . . . either way, you believe in something so extraordinary and magnificent, something that can only be called a miracle. Hence, you are a believer of something bigger and higher than you and me.

As spiritual beings living temporarily in this body, we are less than perfect, thus things like disease will plague us and our loved ones. However, just because disease occurs, until we reach our destiny in the afterlife, does not mean we have to like it. But if we are to get along in life and be happy, we must find a way to accept these shortcomings.

Acceptance is a positive choice, unlike resignation. When you resign yourself to the unwanted situation, it is as if you are surrendering without a fight, becoming a victim instead of a victor. Acceptance requires an acknowledgment of a situation you might not have control over. The difference is that having embraced it, you begin to find solutions and ways to cope and live fully. This active engagement sets a foundation for inner peace, improving overall well-being and self-esteem. Paraphrasing from *Great Expectations*, suffering has taught me that my heart, despite being broken, has now taken on a better shape.

My journey thus far has been fraught with many obstacles and difficulties, which I am sure will continue until the day God calls me home. Nevertheless, I must say that the treacherous road has led me to self-discovery, allowing me to find my true essence. The Parkinson's Diva is a product of this discovery. Although I love to wear beautiful colorful clothing, who I am as a woman with Parkinson's—the Parkinson's Diva—is *not* defined by my exterior appearance. My true essence does not lie in the makeup I wear, the shoes I don, or the clothing I wear. Our beauty should radiate from deep from within our soul, full of hope and gratitude, despite living in a body that has many afflictions.

The essence of any woman with PD is found in loving herself even though she is disease-ridden, body and all. A woman with Parkinson's should not feel the need to hide from anyone because she has a disease. She represents freedom because she knows her worth. This is the essence of one's true self. It is a woman who knows her beauty is beyond the physical and is more valuable than all the precious stones. "She dresses herself with strength and makes her arms strong" (Proverbs 31:17).

One of the reasons I chose the word *diva* to identify myself and other women with Parkinson's is because a person who possesses these traits uses ordinary things and personal limitations to accomplish extraordinary things through divine intervention. This is not unlike what the many stories the Bible teaches us, where God calls on and uses ordinary people to carry out extraordinary tasks (1 Corinthians 1:27). Despite living with twenty-one illnesses, which appear to be increasing in complexity at warp speed, most times when I interact with others, I am frequently questioned if I am truly ill. I guess it is a blessing to look like there is nothing wrong with me. But I realize that it is God's mercy, grace, and peace exponentially multiplied that sustains me—even at my lowest point, when I have no more strength to go on. Peace is the anchor that keeps me steady, even when the world around seems to fall apart.

All of us at this very moment are in the eye of the storm, coming out of a storm, or going into one. This is life. In order not to succumb to fear, anxiety, despair, hopelessness, and cynicism, but rather stay positive and continue smiling, we must make peace with ourselves *just as we are* and let God be.

I don't know if any of you like to dance. I love dancing. I have learned that I don't necessarily have to be a great dancer to truly enjoy dancing, especially if I have a good dancer to lead. When you dance with somebody who knows how to dance and lead, the experience can be magical. It is amazing to me that with the right partner, even on a small dance platform that is jammed-packed, one can glide across the dance floor for hours without once running into anyone. This is the same experience when you let God take lead. Remember:

1. Where He puts you, you will flourish,
2. Where He delivers you from, you will never return,
3. Where He sends you, you will be victorious.

Will you choose fear or faith? The choice is yours. They both demand believing in something one cannot see or touch.

If you find yourself struggling in the dark under pressure, do not fret. You are about to uncover your true worth and rise stronger and more beautiful. Next time you find yourself doubting if you can hold on one more minute, think about the tulip—so fragile, yet it can bloom at minus 20 degrees Fahrenheit, making it extremely resilient as well.

CHAPTER 18

Quizás, Quizás

"'Hope' is the thing with feathers that perches in the soul and sings the tune without the words and never stops at all."

— Emily Dickinson

People, like flowers, bloom in their own time and follow their own individual journeys. Thus, it is important not to compare ourselves to anyone else. The important thing is to be true to yourself.

Think of the lion—he is known as the king of the jungle. But why does he have such a designation? Have you ever wondered? He is neither the fastest, the smartest, nor the biggest animal in the jungle. So, what makes him so special? Simply put, it *all* comes down to his convictions. He is unwavering in his convictions when he makes a stance. He is certain he will be victorious. When he faces any brink, he never backs down or retreats, even in overwhelming opposing odds. This type of fierceness and conviction is what we should all strive to have.

Thus far, this path has proven to be marvelous, although extremely difficult at times. It has allowed me to unveil my true essence of who I am inside. But I still have a few more steps to take. I am not sure where this path will end or how it might twist and turn. However, the important thing is to learn with every step taken *not to fear* but *to walk boldly*, feeling whole. I will live to the fullest, even as I continue to face challenges, knowing victory is ahead with God on my side.

In the end, I deeply believe that all our worldly plights and battles have to do with our destiny, our gifts, and our purpose in this world. We have been entrusted by God with time, opportunities, abilities, and possessions. How we use these is what matters to God. Will we bring glory to Him (God) and help others, or just bury our gifts and never use them, thus missing out on the blessings that they could bring us?

I heard a story once about a young college student whose parents threw her a going-away party. Among the many gifts, there was a Bible. At the time, she did not think this to be a fitting gift and put the book at the bottom of the box she carried with her. For years, she carried this box from apartment to apartment while she took all the contents out of the box . . . and the Bible sat there at the bottom of a book pile, collecting dust. In the meantime, this person had been having financial troubles throughout her college years, always having to scrounge up every little penny, looking under the cushions of the sofa for any loose change, as many of us have done. Until she hit another financial crisis and was not sure what to do . . . and while reflecting on the next move, she saw the Bible there, sitting on the floor underneath a pile of stuff. Because she was desperate for guidance, she picked it up and finally opened it. To her astonishment, there was money stuck between the pages—$1,000.

Many of us go through life not making use of what has been given to us and what is rightfully ours . . . because we don't appreciate these gifts. Thus, we continue struggling.

One thing is for sure, the bigger the tasks we are entrusted with, the greater the challenges we will face in life. So, instead of complaining about our situation, we should be grateful for the gifts and entrustment that has been given to us and ask for guidance on how to use these gifts so that they may bear fruit.

These days, each time I get a new diagnosis, like this last diagnosis which can potentially be life threatening if we don't eradicate it soon, instead of asking *why is this happening to me* and *why can't I be well*, I concentrate on finding out what lesson God is trying to teach me this time around. Could my plight be a benefit to others?

I gather insight and try to learn from the great women leaders and characters of the Bible. Recalling a van Gogh quote, "The heart of a man is very much like the sea, it has its storms, it has its tides and in its depths it has its pearls too." Their courage and faith help me harvest my own pearls.

Like *Hagar*, Abraham's other wife or concubine depending on source, and mother of his first-born son Ishmael, I learned to rely on God's strength to move forward. From *Rebekah*, wife of Isaac, I gleamed that although God's plans may be mysterious, they are always good. I can attest to this since He has always guided my steps, even when I had no clue about what to do or where to go. Just like *Leah*, Jacob's first wife, perseverance through difficult circumstances has been an inspiration in my daily walk with God and in learning to live with dignity with PD, lupus, and a whole host of other illnesses.

Ruth has shown me that seeking God leads to a better life, while *Queen Esther* has taught me to be bold in my daily walk with the Lord and in everything I do. And like *Deborah,* the only female judge in the Bible, I try to face trials with a steadfast commitment, and a fervent faith. From her story, I learned to trust in God and His power, especially when we find ourselves against the wall facing impossible diagnoses, finances, heartbreaks, pains, loneliness, or hopelessness. This is the time to surrender to our Heavenly Father and watch what will happen next. Death is not the end; even dry bones can come back alive if He so wishes.

Despite all my medical setbacks, I am still standing with a heart full of hope and faith. Because we as humans are all intricately intertwined. Each one of us is an integral piece of a big puzzle. When the tapestry of our lives is finished, we should inspire and bring beauty to others.

Start by practicing self-love and begin a connection with a greater power. We all have gifts sitting there to be used at the right time. Once there was a person holding two fishes and five loaves, which was multiplied by Jesus to feed the multitude. And after feeding the crowd, there was still enough to fill twelve more baskets, one for each disciple. This gesture demonstrates the divine power to provide abundantly for our physical and spiritual needs, despite our obvious limitations. The journey can be made palatable and even a veritable joy if we learn to embrace the unknown, accept surprises as part of life and never forget to be grateful, even for the smallest of things. Sometimes the most insignificant things can turn out to be the most memorable treasured gifts, moments, and experiences of our lives.

Challenge yourself out of your comfort zone—expand your brain. The more you know, the more informed decisions you will be able to make. You will also build more brain connections to keep your brain agile.

Always keep your hands open and let go of anger, resentment, and fear—so that you can reach out and take someone else's hand. Only time will tell where this new connection (bond) will take you on your journey. Once I reached out, I found inner beauty, courage, and strength when all I felt and saw was plainness, apprehension, and weakness. The final story is yet to be written. You are the author of your own story—make it exciting and bold and with no regrets.

Don't be afraid to share your story, either. You never know who is listening and what changes it may bring. Be a mentor. Have a support group. I always say we need three people—one to laugh with, one to cry with, and one to talk to. Don't forget to guard your heart, which is believed by many including the Bible to be the seat of the soul. So, you must, ". . . guard your heart, for everything you do flows from it" (Proverbs 4:23).

God does not care about outward appearances, only the state of the heart. It is within the heart of simple, unattractive rocks with hollow interiors where the most precious crystals are built under pressure. Someday, when I am cracked open by God, He will find a precious crystal. I hope to be a beautiful red quartz.

About the Author

Maria L. De León, M.D., is a fellowship-trained movement disorder specialist, patient, caregiver, and passionate advocate for gender equity in healthcare. For over two decades, she has championed women's health, particularly in Parkinson's disease (PD), pioneering research on gender differences in neurological conditions. She played a key role in developing the *Women & PD Initiative* and authored *The Parkinson's Diva*, the first book addressing the unique challenges women face with the disease. Through her work with organizations like the World Parkinson Coalition (WPC), she has helped bridge gaps in care, raise awareness, and advocate for more inclusive research and treatment strategies.

Dr. De León collaborates with leading institutions, including the NIH, FDA, DOD, and the Michael J. Fox Foundation, contributing to research on early PD detection and clinical trial design. She co-authored the first paper on the effects of PD medications on menstruation and developed *In*

Her Shoes, a guide for women living with PD. Committed to empowering Hispanic communities, she works with *Give for a Smile* and the *PD Gene Latino* project to increase representation in genetic research and expand access to care. A recipient of multiple awards, including the 2021 MJFF Public Policy Award, and a two-time finalist for Healthcare Collaborator Champion, Dr. De León continues to be a driving force in the fight for equitable and patient-centered care in Parkinson's disease.

Books by Maria de León, M.D.

The Parkinson's Diva: A Woman's Guide to Parkinson's Disease

Viviendo más allá del párkinson: explorando las posibilidades

Hello, Possibilities! A Journal for Your Daily Walk with Parkinson's Disease

Elegance in Motion: A Parkinson's Diva Journey of Faith and Perseverance

RENOWNED SPEAKER, AUTHOR
AND PATIENT ADVOCATE

www.ingramcontent.com/pod-product-compliance
Lightning Source LLC
Chambersburg PA
CBHW061648120626
46550CB00003B/873